THE BOOK OF
HERBS

NEW YORK

Editor Renny Harrop
Designer Caroline Dewing
Illustrated by Caroline Austin

Published in USA 1985
by Exeter Books
Distributed by Bookthrift
Exeter is a registered trademark of Simon & Schuster
New York, New York

© Marshall Cavendish Limited 1985

ISBN 0-671-07403-2

Printed and bound in Hong Kong by
Dai Nippon Printing Company

INTRODUCTION

Throughout history and throughout the world, herbs have played an important part in the development of mankind. Providing us with food, medicine and cosmetics, herbs can cure, kill and nourish us. In *The Book of Herbs* we have tried to encompass every aspect of their history and use.

The first part of the book describes their history from ancient civilizations to the present day, with reference to mythology, botany, medicine, horticulture and cosmetics. Where possible, we have provided the necessary information to enable you to reproduce the herb gardens, beauty aids, traditional folk remedies and potpourri that enhanced the lives of those who lived in a less complicated age than our own.

The flavor, scent and the medicinal and nutritional properties of fresh herbs are inevitably superior to those of herbs which have been dried or frozen. What better way to provide yourself with a constant supply than to grow them yourself? In the second section of this book we have chosen the most useful herbs and explained how they should be planted and cultivated. It does not matter if you do not have a garden; most herbs grow quite successfully in pots and window boxes. A herb garden will also provide you with a colorful and sweet smelling array of plants that more than compensate for the small amount of time and effort involved in growing them.

In cooking, particularly, herbs come into their own. Mass-produced foods, although convenient, tend also to be bland and boring. The judicious addition of the right herb can help to counter this and add the difference to your cooking which will make it worthy of the best restaurant. The final section includes recipes for family meals and special occasions.

The submergence of many traditional crafts by the development of modern technology is now ending and much knowledge that has been ignored for years is finding new value in our search for simplicity and self sufficiency. We hope that *The Book of Herbs* will help to continue and expand this process in an informative and enjoyable manner.

CONTENTS

HERBS THROUGHOUT HISTORY

As long as man has existed, herbs have been an integral part of his life. Evidence of their use and the traditions which sprang from their consequent importance is still being discovered all over the world.

Before he learned to hunt animals, primitive man depended on plants for both food and medicine. Even after meat became an addition to the human diet, it was for many centuries a luxury and the staple foods were bread and other grain-based products. The only way to give such a regimen variety or savour was by the addition of wild plants—the cultivated vegetable is a comparatively recent introduction. Apart from improving the flavour of food, herbs also helped to preserve it and make it more digestible.

Through experience, a tremendous amount of knowledge on the subject of herbs was gradually accumulated and passed on from one civilization to another. Occasionally this became interwoven with superstition, but even then it was usually based on sound plant lore.

One of the earliest known records of the use of herbs is on an Egyptian papyrus dated about 2000 BC which mentions the existence of herb doctors. Garlic is known to have been fed to the builders of the pyramids to keep them healthy, and other documents illustrate their importance in cooking and religious rites, such as the embalming of the dead. Their knowledge was passed to the Greeks and then to the Romans. Further confirmation of their importance can be found in both the Old and New Testaments of the Bible.

The works of famous Greek philosophers and physicians such as Aristotle and his pupil Hippocrates (in the third century BC), and later of Dioscorides show an extensive knowledge of the botanical nature and medicinal use of hundreds of different kinds of herbs. These works and their influence on the herbals of later botanists cum physicians such as Galen, Tusser, Gerard and Culpeper are discussed in greater detail in the chapter on medicinal herbs, but their influence was far-reaching.

By the time the Romans were making themselves rulers of the world, they depended so much on herbs for cooking and medicine that the Roman armies carried herbs in their baggage on all campaigns and journeys. In the process, sometimes intentionally and sometimes accidentally, they introduced the planting and use of some previously unknown herbs in every part of the Roman Empire. At the same time they also acquired many new herbs themselves from their colonies and incorporated them into their own way of life.

Pliny (23–79 AD) wrote eight books on medicinal plants. Although herbs were used to keep soldiers healthy and treat illness they were by no means restricted to healing. The patrician Romans, particularly, made heavy use of herbs in the rich sauces in which they tended to smother their food. This was in an attempt to disguise the flavour of food which was preserved by salting and drying, often not very satisfactorily. This use of herbs remained until the twentieth century, when refrigeration was invented and had such a radical effect on our eating habits.

While all this was going on in the west, large reference books had also been written in a similar vein in countries such as India and China, where traditional herbal remedies are still prescribed along with more orthodox medicines.

Even after the Roman Empire collapsed, people everywhere continued

Opposite page, above *The herb elecampane is named after Helen of Troy. One legend relates how the plant sprang from the tears she shed after being abducted by Paris.* Opposite page, below *A street vendor selling groundsel.*

6

1591 THE RAPE OF HELEN BY PARIS: BY A FOLLOWER OF FRA ANGELICO ACTIVE 1417 - DIED 1455

to rely on herbs for their flavour, scent and curative properties. Although, in Britain, it took the introduction of Christianity to revive herbs to their former importance after they had fallen into relative obscurity. As monasteries sprang up in Britain and throughout Europe, the monks developed large herb gardens, whose plants were used to cure the sick and revive ailing pilgrims.

Eventually herbs were grown in the gardens of both rich and poor. They were used in the preparation of food, beer, wine, cosmetics, perfumes, candles and insect repellents as well as of medicine. The rich lord would use potions and ungents prepared by his lady to staunch the bleeding and heal the wounds of the men in his private army. The lady herself would strew aromatic herbs among the reeds which covered the floors in an attempt to counter the odours which constantly assailed one in the days before indoor plumbing and sanitation. Herbs used for this purpose were known as 'strewing' herbs.

These early herb gardens were very beautiful as they included plants that we now connect simply with colour and scent, such as carnations, peonies, foxgloves and roses, although in those times every plant had a purpose. For example, as honey was the only form of sweetener, stress was laid on those plants which attracted bees; bergamot, hyssop, balm, lavender, thyme and savory.

By the mid-sixteenth century, the use of herbs was so common that they

7

A sixteenth century apothecary mixing his herbal potions and medicines.

were grown everywhere and the monastery gardens ceased to be so important. Large herb gardens, however, established for the general public for the benefit of their health, such as that in Padua, still survive from this time.

As well as their more functional use, the value of herbs in sometimes determining the difference between life and death, gave them considerable significance in magic and superstition. Astrology was used to work out the most propitious times for the planting and harvesting of herbs. Certain of them were thought to be under the influence of a particular planet—chives, for example, belonged to Mars, and chervil to Jupiter. Even today, some people still plant herbs during the waxing of the moon just to be on the safe side.

Because people knew the power and usefulness of herbs in their everyday life, they turned to them for help against evil and harmful magic. They believed, for example, that rosemary, lavender, dill, hyssop, angelica and southernwood, would protect them from witchcraft and the evil eye. The leaves of the elder were gathered on the last day of April and fixed around doors and windows to protect the inhabitants from charms and spells. The elder was a magic tree, all herbs were under the protection of the elder mother and, although it was full of love for mankind, it was wiser to ask its pardon if forced to cut one down. On the positive side, certain herbs, such as *Artemesia abrotanum* (southernwood), were used to make love potions and charms.

Practical uses, however, included not only their addition to food and medicaments, but their inclusion in pot-pourri and pomanders. These were used to scent yourself and your surroundings and act as a disinfectant. More details about such objects are given on page 16, where we also tell you how to prepare them for yourself.

Oils from the seeds of herbs were used from Roman to Tudor times and beyond to polish wooden floors and furniture. People fortunate enough to posses a bath would add home-made herbal bath additives and the lady of the house would also prepare her own herbal hair rinses and tooth washes in her still room.

The influence and use of herbs was spread from Europe to the New World by the settlers who brought herbs and spices to America from every part of Europe. The Shakers, a sect of Quakers, were among the first to make a commercial success out of growing, drying, packaging and selling herbs.

The popularity of herbs remained reasonably constant until the eighteenth and nineteenth centuries. At this point scientific knowledge became sufficiently advanced for man to evolve synthetic substitutes for many of the properties previously derived from plants. Consequently the use of a vast number of herbs declined and many were cultivated for their beauty and fragrance alone. Perennial favourites such as mint and parsley survived this decline, but generally herbs passed into oblivion.

In recent years, science has helped reverse this situation by proving the nutritional and medicinal value of plants and incorporating them into modern medicines and cosmetics. Simultaneously, although food has ceased to necessitate the use of herbs to preserve and disguise its flavour, mass production and its consequent detrimental effect on the taste of food, has ensured the revival of herbs in the kitchen. All the information needed to grow herbs for these purposes is contained in the Concise Herbal section of this book, while the final section is devoted to recipes in which the herbs have been chosen to complement the main ingredients.

Socially, along with our increased capacity for self-destruction, there has evolved an increasing awareness of our ecology and environment, leading to a greater appreciation and reliance on natural products. Interest in herbs is consequently reviving as people return to the cultivation and use of plants in every aspect of their lives.

HERBS FOR HEALTH

Herbs have always contributed a great deal to human health, and they still do. Their most obvious value is as the source of some of the drugs and medicines used in modern remedies. For example, pyrethrum is made from a member of the chrysanthemum family. From the poppy comes opium and heroine and the pain-killer morphine. Digitalin, the drug used for heart disorders, is derived from the leaves of the foxglove. Indeed until comparatively recently herbs were the major source of medicines, for when antibiotics and other such modern drugs were unknown, people were forced to rely upon natural tried and tested cures.

Herbalists

The first known important work, however, dealing specifically with medicinal herbs was written by a Greek physician, Dioscorides. In about 60 AD he compiled a herbal called *De Materia Medica*. The book described the properties of some six hundred plants. The information was so complete and so accurate that the herbal was used as a standard text for centuries afterwards.

One of those who used Dioscorides' herbal as a work of reference was Willian Turner, who lived from 1508 to 1579. Turner, a Protestant clergyman, a doctor of medicine and the pioneer figure in English botany, was a scientist by training. The *Herball* he wrote shows the mixture in him of curiosity and strict caution.

John Gerard, who was born in 1545 in Nantwich, Cheshire, England, and wrote what is probably the most famous of all herbals, did not have Turner's strictness. His book expresses above all his enthusiastic love of plants. Even so, its warmth does not diminish Gerard's scientific insight and discipline. During his lifetime he was a surgeon, the superintendent of Lord Burghley's gardens (Lord Burghley was Elizabeth I's Chief Secretary of State) and an apothecary to James I. And as a physician and gardener he made a collection of seeds and plants from gardens throughout Europe, even employing a plant collector to find new items.

Below A *detail of the poppy plant, from which opium, heroine and morphine are extracted.* Bottom left A *woodcut showing the stylized nature of early herbal illustrations.* Bottom right A *detail of the foxglove from which the drug digitalis is extracted for use in the treatment of heart conditions.*

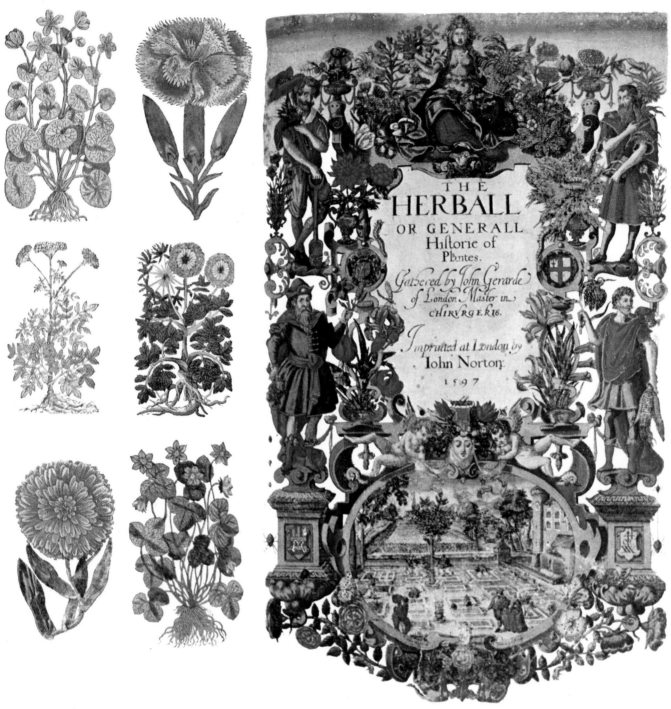

The frontispiece and some of the illustrations from Gerard's Herbal, published in 1597.

A later herbal, which makes fascinating reading, is that published by Nicholas Culpeper in 1649. His book is particularly interesting because at that time medical treatment was extremely expensive and poorer people were forced to treat themselves by using simples, or remedies made from herbs gathered wild or grown outside their cottages. Culpeper's book was intended to supply these people with all the information necessary to treat themselves without recourse to doctors.

Culpeper linked herbs with astrology and tended to exaggerate the medicinal claims to be made for each plant. He was also an advocate of a system of natural healing, still found all over the world, called the Doctrine of Signatures. This system works on the basis that 'like cures like': yellow plants cure liverish conditions, such as jaundice, which tinges the skin yellow; plants with heart-shaped leaves are good for the heart; plants with red flowers or blotches of red on their stems or leaves are good for the blood, and so on. This doctrine resulted in many herbs being named after the specific medicinal properties they were held to have, such as eyebright, liverwort (agrimony) and heartsease.

In 1694, nearly a hundred years after Gerard's death, John Pechey published his *Compleat Herbal of Physical Plants*. He, too, was a doctor who had absorbed both the old learning and the new explorations in botanical science.

For these men, and for many others like them with a rigorous scientific training, there was an obvious connection between herbs and health.

Herbal medicine has, of course, never disappeared. There are still homeopathic pharmacies and certainly people still use traditional herbal cures. In China there have grown up two entirely separate schools of medicine, one centred around modern western drugs and surgical techniques and the other based upon acupuncture and traditional mainly herbal medicines—some of which have remained virtually unchanged for 2,700 years. Recently, too, in the west there has been a drift back to 'natural' cures and herbal medicines in reaction against the ever-increasing complexity of modern drugs.

Medicinal teas

The various herb teas are really the safest, easiest and best ways of getting the benefit from aromatic leaves and flowers of herbs. The majority of these teas are also anti-indigestive and relaxing—the preparation and merits of herbal teas, or tisanes, are given in detail on page 26.

Herbal medicines

Making your own medicines can be a complicated and somewhat hazardous occupation because many of the herbs have dangerous or unexpected side-effects. So anyone interested would be wise not to attempt to it but to investigate the stock of the nearest herbal or homeopathic supplier. Among other things a number of creams and ointments are made from herbs, one well known one being comfrey ointment which has quite amazingly good effects in cases of back strain. (In medieval times this herb was called boneset or knitbone, and recommended for sprains and strained backs.)

Herbal medicine becomes further confused because each herb was used to cure innumerable ailments. Rue, for example, which is dangerous taken in large quantities, was used for putting on bee and wasp srtings, as an antidote for poisons, as a cure for dizziness and to take away warts and pimples.

Some herbal cures

Many of the herbal cures do now seem rather fanciful. The very few listed below are included for their interest value, you are not really advised to try them.

Asthma sufferers, even as late as the first quarter of the twentieth century, were advised to 'mince garlic, spread it on thin bread and butter, and eat just before going to bed'.

At the same time a dandruff cure, which unfortunately is not specific about the quantity of sage in a packet, or how to dissolve it, recommended that you 'Take one packet and a half of sage, and dissolve it in one pint of boiling water. When cold, strain into a bottle and brush into the scalp every night'. (If you do consider trying this be careful, the sage liquid will stain walls and clothes, and may, like some hair-colourants, temporarily stain your scalp!)

Two particularly odd herbal cures state that to improve a bad memory you should drink sage tea, sweetened to taste, and that garlic sliced and worn in the socks will cure rheumatism.

To keep your skin clear some herbalists advise you to boil elder flowers in water, strain and then drink the liquid. And a nice seventeenth-century recipe for 'An excellent water for Ye sight' says: 'Take fennel, anniseed

Part of a homeopathic dispensary, where herbs are used, among other naturally available plants and minerals, to make remedial medicines.

and elecampane, dry and powder them, mix in good brandy, dry it again; every morning and evening eate a pretty quantity, it is excellent for sight'. While another of the same period tells you to 'Take a good white wine, infuse eyebright in it three dayse, then seethe it with a little rosemary, drink if often, it is most excellent to restore and strengthen the sight. Also eate of the powder of eyebright in a new laid egg rare-roasted every morning'.

A Welsh antidote for a spider's bite was to mix garlic, treacle and ale—unfortunately the quantities are not given. But you were supposed to drink freely of the mixture so ale probably predominated.

There are many complicated and expensive recipes for removing freckles and sunburn, mostly dating from the times when a pale skin was the sign of a lady. Rather more useful ones are those which tell you how to stop sunburn hurting. One such advises washing the affected part with sage tea. Finally, a delightful recipe for 'Comforting the head and the braine' which says: 'Take rosemary and sage of both sorts of both, with flowers of rosemary if to be had, and borage with ye flowers. Infuse in good Canary wine for three days, drink it often.'

The medicinal herbs

The medicinal properties of herbs were second in importance only to the culinary qualities. Below are listed the traditional medicinal usages and beliefs attributed to various herbs—obviously not all the reputed curative properties are to be relied upon or tested.

Agrimony This is an ancient medicinal herb. The Greeks used it to cure cataract. In Britain, many centuries later, it was made into a spring tonic and a blood purifier which was 'good for them that heave naughty livers'.

Agrimony was also made into an ointment called *arquebused* and applied to wounds inflicted by an arquebus, a hand-held gun.

Bergamot Because, like all the mints, it contains thymol, bergamot used to be made into an infusion for colds and sore throats.

It is only quite recently that its qualities as a tea have been discovered in Europe, but they have been famous for centuries in the northern part of the United States, and in Canada. The Oswego Indians must have been the first to use its leaves to make a tea, for in North America this plant is named after them. After the 'Boston Tea Party', (December 16, 1773) patriotic American colonists drank it instead of Indian Tea.

Its fragrance when it is growing makes it a good bee plant and one of its American names is bee balm.

Betony This was ground into an ointment with hog's grease and used to soothe burns.

Borage Even in Roman times, borage had the reputation of being a cheerful, encouraging plant, one that, in Pliny's words, 'brings always courage'.

Centuries later, the great Elizabethan gardener and herbalist, John Gerard had the same praise for it in its use 'for the comfort of the heart, to drive away sorrow'. He—and many other people—had found that the effect of its leaves in a salad was 'to exhilarate and make the mind glad', and the idea of an exhilarating salad is delicious in itself.

Borage was grown, too, for the beauty of its vivid blue flowers—Louis XIV had some planted in the gardens of Versailles—and they have been much copied in embroidery for centuries.

Catmint, Catnip The true catmint is *Nepeta cataria* which, said John Gerard, cats love so much that 'they rub themselves upon it, wallow or tumble in it, and also feed upon the branches and leaves very greedily'. People like it very well too—as a medicine. It was regarded as 'a present help for them that be bursten inwardly of some fall received from a high place'. That makes it sound more a miracle than a medicine, but 'bursten inwardly' was just a vivid version of 'bruise'.

Below Aniseed, *mixed with* fennel, elecampane *and brandy, was recommended to be taken twice a day to improve the sight.* Bottom *Sprigs of flowering* borage, *added to* sage *and* rosemary *and infused in Canary wine, was said to comfort the head and brain.*

Chervil This is yet another herb which the Romans brought into Europe from the shores of the Mediterranean and the Levant.

In England in the fifteenth century it was an essential plant, and it stayed in favour. For John Gerard, chervil made salads that excelled 'in wholesomeness for the cold and feeble stomache'. The boiled roots were a preventative against plague. It could be eaten to cure the hiccups, and its leaves soothed the pain of rheumatism and bruises.

Chives One of the most ancient of all herbs, chives were a favourite in China as long ago as 3000 BC. They were enjoyed for their mild, delicious onion flavour, and used as an antidote to poison and to stop bleeding. For a herb, chives came late to the gardens of Europe, arriving in the sixteenth century.

Coltsfoot Its odd country name, son-before-father, was given to it because the flowers appear before the leaves. For many centuries coltsfoot (or coughwort) flowers have been valued for their use in treating various chest complaints, particularly bronchitis and asthma. They were dried and then inhaled or smoked, and have been used as a substitute for tobacco, too.

Comfrey There is a tradition that comfrey was much grown in the herb gardens of monasteries. That may have been because monks so often had to care for the sick and injured, and one of the old names for comfrey was knit-bone.

It was believed to mend broken bones, and to heal such things as bruises, sprains, swellings and backache. One Elizabethan recipe is for comfrey root, boiled in sugar and liquorice, and mixed with coltsfoot, mallow and poppy seeds to make an ointment for curing bad backs and strains. But its use was not confined to muscular troubles, people also made comfrey tea for colds and bronchitis, using 25g/1oz of dried leaves to 600ml/1 pint (2½ cups) of boiling water.

Dill The common name comes from the Norse word *dilla*, meaning 'lull'— dill was believed to be good for insomnia. The seed is used as a mild medicine for flatulence, good for soothing a 'windy' baby.

Elder Elderflower water has been taken as a remedy for colds for several centuries.

Elecampane The botanical name, *Inula Helenium*, comes from Helen of Troy. There is a legend that the plant sprang from her tears, but John Gerard says that her hands were full of it when Paris took her away from Greece.

Elecampane looks like a sunflower, and in Germany there was an ancient custom of putting a bunch of it in the centre of a nosegay of herbs to symbolize the sun and the head of Odin, the greatest of the Norse gods.

The Romans, in their practical way, used the roots in a medicine for the cure of over-eating, and Tudor herbalists candied them to use for the treatment of coughs, catarrhs, bronchitis, and chest ailments generally.

Eyebright The botanical name, *Euphrasia officinalis*, comes from Euphrosyne, one of the three Graces, whose name is the Greek word for gladness, and the common name comes from its use as an eye lotion. Milton in *Paradise Lost*, speaks of how it was used with rue to restore Adam's sight.

Long ago, country people used to use it, too, for an early morning drink, and in some places they made wine from it. In the north of England, where it grows on Hadrian's Wall, it was used to treat hay fever.

Fennel The Greeks thought very highly of fennel and used it for slimming and for treating more than twenty different illnesses. The Romans ate it—root, leaf and seed—in salads and baked it in bread and cakes. In Anglo-Saxon times it was used on fasting days, presumably because, as the Greeks had already discovered, it stilled the pangs of hunger. Even in later centuries it was 'much used in drink to make people more lean that are too fat'.

In the Middle Ages fennel was a favourite strewing herb, for, apart from

Below An infusion of dill water has been a traditional remedy for flatulence for centuries. Bottom As well as having a mild and delicious oniony flavour, which makes the chive a great asset in cooking, it has also been used as an antidote to poisons and to stop bleeding.

Below *The origin of the common name for* Marrubium vulgare, *horehound, is derived from its use as an antidote to the bight of a mad dog.* Bottom *An old manuscript showing an illustration of vervain.*

being fragrant, it kept insects at bay. It had a high place in the kitchen, too, lending its flavour to food that was often far from fresh to make it palatable. The royal household of Edward I, who reigned in England towards the end of the thirteenth century, used fennel at the rate of 3.8kg/8½lbs each month.

Fennel even had power against witches. If it were hung over the doorway on Midsummer Eve it would keep them away. And people who put it in the keyhole of their bedrooms made sure that nothing dangerous would disturb their sleep.

Garlic This is one of the oldest and most valued of all cultivated plants. It may have come into southern Europe from the east. Certainly it was known to the Ancient Egyptians who used it as a food and a medicine and thought so highly of it that it seemed almost a god to them. The builders of the pyramids ate it; the Children of Israel ate it; the Romans—needless to say—ate it and encouraged other people to do the same. It was an ingredient in medicine for leprosy—the term for a leper in the Middle Ages was pilgarlic, because he had to peel his own.

The antiseptic quality of garlic is not just a matter of faith—in World War I, sphagnum moss soaked in garlic juice was used for wound dressings. Garlic was valued in other medicines, too, for the digestion and for colds, coughs and asthma, and an old country remedy for whooping cough was to put a clove of garlic in the shoes of the whooper!

Horehound The Greeks thought highly of it and used it as an antispasmodic drug. It was an antidote, too, for the bite of a mad dog, and this, of course, is how it got its common name.

Lemon balm *Melissa offinalis*, the botanical name for this herb, comes from the Greek word for 'bee' and the Greeks believed that bees would never go away from a hive if it grew nearby. The hives were even rubbed with it to make the bees welcome.

Lemon balm had valuable qualities for human beings, too. It soothed tension. It was a dressing for wounds, especially sword wounds, and in the Middle Ages it was believed that a sprig of lemon balm placed on an injury was enough to staunch the blood. It was good for the ears, toothache, and sickness during pregnancy. It was held to cure mad dog bites, skin eruptions and crooked necks. It prevented baldness. And when made into an amulet in a piece of linen or silk, it caused the women who wore it to be beloved and happy.

With all these powers to its credit, it is not surprising that the Ancient Greeks believed that it promoted long life, and that a Prince Llewellyn of Glamorgan drank 'mellissa tea'—so he claimed—every day of the 108 years of his life.

Lovage The Greeks used lovage for a medicine and so did the Romans. It was they who brought it to Britain and spread it about Central Europe.

Lovage was grown all through the 'Dark Ages'. It is yet another of the almost-all-purpose medicines: it was taken for sore throats, quinsy, and for eye ailments; for indigestion and stomach-ache, and for getting rid of boils, spots and freckles. It was also added to baths, most probably as the earliest deodorant.

In Central Europe, when girls went to meet their lovers, they wore lovage in a bag hanging round their necks, and perhaps it was its use as a perfume that led to lovage being put into love potions which were guaranteed to awaken everlasting devotion.

Pennyroyal The Romans gave pennyroyal the name *Mentha pulegium* for it kept away fleas, and *pulex* is the Latin for flea. The great John Gerard called this pudding grass. In Tudor times it was gathered in London among the marshy parts of 'Miles end . . . poore women being plenty to sell it in London markets'.

Maybe the 'poore women' of Gerard's day found a ready market for it because it had so many uses. Gerard himself claimed that it would purify

'Corrupt water' on sea voyages, and that it would cure 'swimming in the head and the paines and giddiness thereof'. And in dried and powdered form it was made into medicine for coughs and colds.

Rocket This must have been an early form of anaesthetic. The Romans—who sometimes sound like travelling herbalists in chariots—ate both the leaves and the seeds, and the Elizabethans were also extremely partial to it. One herbalist recommended its being taken before a whipping, so that the pain would not be felt, and another praised its use against the biting of the shrew mouse 'and other venomous beasts'!

St. John's wort St. John was the patron saint of horses and this herb was reputed to cure equine ailments.

Sage Sage was yet another traveller to Britain and northern Europe in the Roman baggage train. Its Latin name, *salvia* means 'health', and from very early times people believed that it was a source of well-being, both physical and mental.

The Greeks used it to counteract all manner of afflictions, including ulcers, consumption, snake bites and grief. The Romans ate it. The Chinese at one time preferred sage tea to 'tea' tea, partly for its tonic properties. It was held to be good for the brain, the senses and the memory—it strengthened the sinews; it was good for palsy and cured stitches; it made a good gargle and mouthwash and kept the teeth white. And Gerard recommended its use in the brewing of ale!

Savory Savory was grown in Egypt in ancient times, and used in love potions. The Romans liked it, too, but they used it in a spicy sauce. When it became at home in Europe, it was used chiefly as a medicine, for cheering people up, for tired eyes, for ringing in the ears, for indigestion, for wasp and bee stings, and for other shocks to the system.

Tansy This herb was used as a popular cure for worms and also to bring on abortion.

Tarragon *Artemisia dracunculus* is the botanical name and *dracunculus* means, charmingly, little dragon. In ancient times, the mixed juices of tarragon and fennel made a favourite drink of the rulers of India. In the reign of Henry VIII, the little dragon made its way into English gardens, and the diarist John Evelyn described it as 'friendly to the head, heart, and liver'.

Thyme A tisane made from the leaves of this herb is supposed to cure insomnia.

Wormwood Its grand name first, according to tradition, was *Parthenis absinthum*, but Artemis, the Greek goddess of chastity, had so much benefit from it that she gave it her name and it became *Artemisia absinthum*. There is even more to its name, for its bitter taste is proverbial, and *absinthum* means 'destitute of delight'.

Wormwood was well thought of as a medicine for a number of complaints. It was used to cure quinsy, prevent drunkeness, and heal the bites of rats and mice, and, mixed with wine, rosemary, blackthorn and saffron, it had a reputation for keeping people in good health. Wormwood had its magical qualities, too. If it was hung beside the door, it kept away evil spirits. And, back in the everyday world, if it was added to ink, it stopped mice from eating old letters.

Valerian Also known as 'all heal', a tisane made from this herb is supposed to act as a general panacea.

Yarrow The botanical name of a herb very often tells much of its early history—or maybe its early legend. Yarrow got its botanical name, *Achillea millefolium*, because it was the herb used by the Greek hero Achilles to heal his warriors in the Trojan War. An old country name for it is 'soldiers' woundwort', and it was chiefly famed and used for its healing qualities, probably in the form of an ointment. In infusions it was taken as a tonic and a cure for feverish colds. People did try it, too, as a cure for baldness, though its efficacy is not proven.

An illustration from a thirteenth century manuscript showing a man suffering from the bite of a mad dog, below him, and on the right, henbane, the plant used to cure him.

HERBS FOR BEAUTY

Herbs have been used in cosmetics for thousands of years—even the ancient Egyptians developed their own rouge and lip-reddener from plant extracts. Unfortunately, however, they were largely superseded by mass-produced synthetic products which could be manufactured with greater speed and economy but were inevitably less pure.

Recently there has been a return by commercial cosmetic firms to incorporating herbs in their products, reflecting a general trend towards a more natural, uncomplicated way of life. But although it is possible to buy many herbal beauty aids, it is so simple and economical to make them yourself that it is worth experimenting with a few recipes.

It has been possible to rediscover the original formulae for many of the old beauty preparations because careful houswives wrote them down in their family recipe books, many of which have survived to this day. As you experiment with them you will be able to invent new concoctions suited to your individual requirements.

Whether you grow your own herbs or buy them makes little difference, although the fresher they are the better. Some cosmetics require whole herbs, while others are based on herbal infusions or herbal oil, that is the essential or volatile oil contained in the leaves and/or flowers. These oils have the property of improving the circulation of the blood, encouraging the production of white corpuscles and acting as a disinfectant. Where a concentrated oil is required, this must be bought from a herbalist as the quantity of herbs necessary to extract oil makes this an impractical project for the home herbalist. Although initially these may be expensive, the quantities needed in the preparations are so minute that the oil becomes a long term investment.

It is worth remembering that herbal cosmetics only work externally. It is equally important to eat properly and take regular exercise. The use of herbs and good fresh vegetables and fruit in your diet is as important to beauty as the use of them in cosmetics.

How to make a herbal infusion

Pour boiling water over the appropriate herb and leave to infuse as you would if making tea. The proportion should be either 3-4 tablespoons of fresh herbs, or 1 teaspoon of dried herbs, to 300ml/10floz (1¼ cups) of boiling water. Use an earthenware or china pot but not one made of metal and leave the infusion to steep for at least 30 minutes before straining and bottling in screw-top jars. An infusion will keep in the refrigerator for a week. Never waste it, if you have made more than you require for a specific recipe, the remainder can be added to your bath water.

The face

The three basic steps to keeping your skin firm and supple are cleansing, toning and moisturizing. Cleansing entails removing the grime and dirt from your skin, which accumulates every day, especially if you live or work in a city. This tends to open the pores slightly. Consequently, the next step is to tone the skin. Toners, or tonics, are mildly astringent and close the pores up again and firm the skin. Inevitably both cleansers and tonics tend to dry the skin slightly and remove some of the natural oils. These are replaced by moisturizers which keep the skin supple and help to prevent wrinkles. Once a week you should clean your face thoroughly. This can be achieved either by a facial steam bath or by using a face pack or mask. Do not use these methods too often, unless you have some persistent blemishes, as they dry the skin.

Facial steam baths

Put two cups of herbs in a bowl with 1 litre/2 pints (5 cups) of boiling water. Hold your face over the bowl and cover your head with a towel to make a tent. Steam your face, keeping it about 30cm/1ft from the bowl for 4 to 8 minutes. Chamomile, elder flowers, yarrow, fennel, sage and lime flowers are suitable for this purpose.

Face packs

Method 1 Chop three or four handfuls of fresh herbs, put them into a pan and just cover with boiling water. Simmer for about 10 minutes or until the leaves combine to make a thick mash. Set aside to cool a little. While

The increase in the popularity of herbal cosmetics reflects the general trend towards a more natural way of living. Although commercial herbal products are available, it is much cheaper to make your own. Pure cosmetics, applied regularly, will help your skin and hair, but remember to eat properly as well.

Chamomile flowers made into a shampoo or herbal rinse not only act as a conditioner but also lighten fair hair.

it is still warm, spread it over a pad of sterile cotton (available in boxes) and apply this to your face, avoiding the eyes and mouth. Leave on for 10 to 15 minutes. Rinse off with lukewarm water.

Sage, or a mixture of dandelion and nettle leaves, are both particularly good for this sort of pack, but any of the herbs recommended for a facial steam bath would be suitable.

Method 2 Mix a small carton of yogurt, 150ml/5floz ($\frac{1}{2}$ cup), with 1 teaspoon of infused fennel seeds and 1 teaspoon of fresh, chopped fennel leaves. Spread evenly over your face, avoiding the eyes and mouth. Leave for 10 to 15 minutes and then rinse off with lukewarm water.

Fennel acts as both a tonic and a wrinkle smoother.

N.B. As when using any form of face mask or pack, be careful to protect your eyes with cotton wool balls soaked in cold water.

Cleansers

These should be used every morning and evening. A good basic cleanser is an investment.

Basic cleansing cream The cleansing agent in this cream is the lanolin. Both lanolin and beeswax are obtainable from dispensing chemists (drugstores). Use this cream to clean your skin night and morning: apply a small amount, massage it well into the skin, then remove all traces with a clean tissue.

	Metric/U.K.	U.S.
Beeswax	14g/$\frac{1}{2}$oz	1 Tbs
Lanolin	25g/1oz	2 Tbs
Avocado or olive oil	75ml/3floz	$\frac{3}{8}$ cup
Herbal water (infusion of the appropriate herb)	2 Tbs	2 Tbs
Essential herb oil (for scent)	2 drops	2 drops

Melt the beeswax with the lanolin in a double saucepan over low heat. When they are completely liquid stir in the oil. Remove the saucepan from the heat and stir in the herbal water and essential oil. Stir constantly until cool. Keep the cream in a screw-top jar.

Skin toners

Face tonics or toners are basically cold teas, the 'infusions' described at the beginning of this chapter. They should be patted on to the cleansed skin with a tissue or cotton ball and left to dry. Apart from closing the pores, some herbs have other beneficial effects.

Chamomile Tones up relaxed muscles.

Comfrey An infusion of comfrey, especially if mixed with witch hazel water helps smooth wrinkles and is a tonic.

Elder An infusion of the leaves or flowers has a slight bleaching effect and helps fade blotches and freckles.

Fennel An infusion of leaves or seeds helps clear spots as fennel has healing properties.

Lady's mantle Particularly good for sensitive skins.

Lemon balm Helps smooth wrinkles.

Lime flowers Helps smooth wrinkles.

Mint An infusion of mint sprigs is quite a strong astringent and is excellent for cleansing ingrained dirt and spots. If your skin is particularly sensitive only half the amount of herbs should be used to that recommended in the introduction to this chapter.

Nettle An infusion of nettle leaves is good for tired skin as it is astringent and gives a refreshing tingle.

Rosemary A tonic which brightens up sagging skin.

Tansy Infused with buttermilk instead of water, tansy has a slight bleaching effect and helps fade freckles.

Thyme Reasonably astringent and helps to clear spots and acne.
Yarrow Astringent, good for greasy skins.
For a stronger astringent effect, any of these herbal infusions may be mixed with witch hazel water.

Moisturizers

Having cleansed and toned your skin, you should then apply a moisturizer. Any plain, unscented cold cream can be easily turned into a fragrant herbal cream. You can just add chopped herb leaves to the cream—but you may find it difficult to remove the little pieces of herb from your face! Or you could heat the cold cream up gently in a pan and add a little herb oil to it. Alternatively for the more adventurous you could try the following recipe.

Night moisturizing cream
Use a very little at a time and leave it on your face overnight.

	Metric/U.K.	U.S.
Beeswax	50g/2oz	$\frac{1}{4}$ cup
Cocoa butter	25g/1oz	2 Tbs
Avocado oil	5 Tbs	5 Tbs
Distilled water	4 Tbs	4 Tbs
Wheat germ oil	1$\frac{1}{2}$ Tbs	1$\frac{1}{2}$ Tbs
Borax	$\frac{3}{4}$ tsp	$\frac{3}{4}$ tsp

Melt the beeswax, cocoa butter and avocado oil in a double saucepan over low heat. When they are completely liquid and well blended, stir in the distilled water, wheat germ oil and borax. Whip the mixture until it cools to prevent granules forming.

Eye lotions

Eye baths are restoring to tired eyes and helpful in cases of conjunctivitis and eye strain. A cold infusion of any of the following herbs will help clear bloodshot eyes; parsley, elderflowers, dried cornflowers, verbena, fennel and eyebright. If you can find or buy eyebright, it is by far the most effective.

Teeth

Fresh sage leaves, rubbed on the teeth, whiten and cleanse them, as well as strengthening the gums. Eating fresh strawberries also whitens the teeth because of the acid they contain.

Hair

Herbs can help give lustre and body to the hair and may be incorporated into both shampoos and conditioning rinses.

Herbal shampoos One of the most natural and refreshing ways of washing your hair is to use a home-made herbal shampoo. Herbal shampoos are made quite simply by pouring boiling water over fresh or dried herbs, leaving them to steep for 24 hours, and then straining off the liquid. The usual measure is about one heaped teaspoon of herbs (or more if using fresh herbs) to one cup of water, but a slightly stronger brew will do no harm at all. Add the infusion to a mild baby shampoo.

However, if you want to make an entirely home-made herbal shampoo, you will need another herb—soapwort. This common and attractive perennial grows in hedges, by streams and on damp waste ground. The pink, scented flowers appear in late summer and the leaves, from which the soapy substance is drawn, are broadly elliptical and strongly veined.

For centuries before the advent of commercial soap, the plant was used by country people for all washing purposes—and at one time it was particularly recommended for washing delicate silks because it gave them a sheen which could be achieved in no other way. The strongest concen-

Below Rubbing fresh sage leaves on the teeth helps clean and whiten them as well as strengthening the gums. Bottom Most commercial shampoos contain detergent, which does little good to your hair and the only purpose of which is to produce vast quantities of foam. By making your own shampoo you can ensure that this undesirable substance is removed and that only the health-giving qualities of whatever herb you have selected are present.

tration of the soapy substance is in the root, but it is not very practical to use it because you will destroy the whole plant. The leaves and stems should be sufficient—and are available dried.

Although herbal shampoos can now be bought it is much cheaper and more satisfactory to make your own, and you will be sure that, unlike commercially-made shampoos, they contain no detergent.

When making the shampoo avoid using metal containers as these will mar the fragrance. Use small china or pottery vessels with tight-fitting cork lids, a wooden spoon and a nylon strainer.

Be sure to buy purified borax (available in chemists and drugstores) and not the kind recommended for laundering or cleaning sinks.

Basic shampoo If you are using fresh herbs—which are always preferable if available—gently bruise the leaves before making the infusion to allow as much of the essence as possible to mingle with the water.

	Metric/U.K.	U.S.
Dried soapwort (or one handful of fresh leaves and stems)	2 Tbs	2 Tbs
Chamomile flowers	1 Tbs	1 Tbs
Borax	1 tsp	1 tsp

Divide the ingredients equally into two china or pottery jars. Fill each jar with 300ml/10floz (1¼ cups) boiling water. Wedge the corks in tightly and leave the mixture to steep for about 24 hours. Give the jars a good shake from time to time. Pour the mixture through a nylon strainer and discard the herbs.

Variations

Anti-dandruff shampoo If you are troubled by dandruff add an infusion of one part stinging nettle and one part parsley to the shampoo above.

Perfumed shampoos A few lime flowers or two sprigs of lavender added to the basic shampoo before corking will give your hair a delicate, natural fragrance.

Bear in mind that this natural shampoo will not be nearly as 'soapy' as a commercial shampoo. People tend to believe that a shampoo will only clean their hair properly if it produces a tremendous lather, which is why so many commercial shampoos contain detergents which do just that (and little else). A mild and gentle herbal shampoo cannot compete so far as froth goes—but its cleansing and aromatic qualities are undeniable.

Herbal rinses and conditioners

Herbal rinses are simply made by infusing the herb of your choice in water as described at the beginning of this chapter. All of the herb rinses mentioned, if poured over the hair as a final rinse after shampooing, will make your hair shine, but some of them have additional properties.

An infusion of nettles, lime flowers, fennel or sage will act as a good general conditioner.

A parsley rinse helps clear dandruff, and is also reputed to restore thickness to thinning hair.

A rosemary rinse darkens dark hair and imparts a delicious fragrance.

An infusion of chamomile flowers brightens fair hair and has the reputation of stimulating hair growth.

It is, of course, possible to combine one or more herbs together, such as nettle and rosemary, and infuse them to make a hair rinse to suit your individual requirements.

Feet

An infusion of marigold or lime flowers or lavender leaves added to a hot foot bath will refresh tired feet. After the bath, dry your feet and rub them with the essential oil of marigold petals to get rid of any soreness.

Hands

Always try to remember to wear rubber gloves for washing up and rub hand cream into your hands whenever they have been immersed in water or exposed to inclement weather. Below is a recipe to enable you to make your own herbal hand cream.

Hand cream

	Metric/U.K.	U.S.
Glycerine	50g/2oz	$\frac{1}{4}$ cup
Elderflower water	75ml/3floz	$\frac{1}{3}$ cup
Essential oil of lavender, roses		
or bergamot	12 drops	12 drops
Lemon juice	8 drops	8 drops

Mix together the glycerine and elderflower water. Stir in the herbal oil and lemon juice and store in a screw-top jar.

Bathing

Any aromatic herb added to the bathwater in oil, vinegar or bag form, will scent and refresh the body. Particular herbs, however, have special

Left Fresh or dried herbs may be used in the preparation of shampoos, handcreams and bath oils. Right, below The essential oil extracted from lavender makes a sweet-smelling additive to herbal hand cream. Right, bottom Any aromatic herb added to bath water will scent and refresh the body.

properties, and it is from these that we suggest you make your selection:

Agrimony and **ragwort** are both recommended for aching muscles.

Lovage has a pleasant aroma and acts as a mild deodorant.

Angelica acts as a skin stimulant.

Comfrey and **rosemary** Prolonged immersion in bath water infused with either of these two herbs is said to rejuvenate the skin.

Valerian and **chamomile** have a soporific effect and are ideal for evening baths.

Southernwood, with its lemony tang, **nettle** leaves or well-boiled **juniper** roots are all invigorating.

Eucalyptus leaves, **rosemary, lavender, elderflowers, rose, geranium** leaves and **violets** will all provide a particularly fragrant bath.

There are many ways to add herbs to the bath, which incidentally is a very ancient tradition, the point to remember is *never to throw herbs directly into the water*, or you will have to spend hours trying to clean the bath out and the waste pipe may become blocked.

Infusions Prepare as specified in the introduction to this chapter and add directly to the bath water in whatever quantity you like.

Essential oils may be bought and added directly to the bath water drop by drop until it is sufficiently scented, or make your own oil.

Bath oils Prepare according to the following recipe and add directly to the bath water.

For the oil use either olive, sunflower, safflower, sesame seed, avocado or almond. Choose herbs from the recommended list or use mint or pine needles for a particularly invigorating bath. Pour 600ml/1 pint (2½ cups) of oil into a large pottery or china bowl. Add as many fresh flowers or leaves as it will take and cover. Soak for a couple of days. Remove, strain, squeeze out and discard the flowers or leaves. Add as many fresh herbs as possible to the remaining oil and leave for a further two days. Repeat the removal and addition of herbs until you have used about ten batches. (This is why herbal oils are so expensive to buy.) Always keep the bowl covered. Finally strain the oil, squeezing the herbs firmly and then discarding them, and store the oil in tightly capped or corked bottles in a dark cool place.

Bath vinegars

These are more astringent than bath oils and are more suitable if you have a greasy skin. Select herbs from the recommended list with the addition of bergamot and balm. Take two cups of fresh leaves or flowers and when they have been washed and dried, pack them loosely in a wide-mouthed glass jar. Pour over 1 litre/2 pints (5 cups) of wine or cider vinegar. Cover tightly and place the jar where you will remember to shake it, or stir the contents with a wooden spoon, every other day. After ten days, rub a little on the skin and smell. If it is not herby enough, drain the herbs away and replace with fresh leaves or flowers and repeat the process. When the vinegar is ready, strain it into bottles, add a sprig of the appropriate herb for decoration and cap tightly. One cupful of herbal vinegar per bath should be adequate.

Bath bags

Bath bags are simple to make, provide an instant infusion and are re-usable. Cut a piece of cheesecloth or muslin 20cm/8in square. Fill the centre with one or more herbs selected from the recommended list. Take up the corners of the cheesecloth and tie together firmly with ribbon or string. Either attach the bag to the tap so that it is hit by the hot running water, or simply place it in the bath and pour very hot or boiling water over it. Fill up the bath and use the bag to scrub yourself with. When the herbs have been exhausted, untie the bag and discard them. Rinse out the cheesecloth and refill with fresh herbs.

A few sprigs of fresh or dried soapwort added to the bath bag will give the water a gentle cleansing effect.

Below Sunflower oil is highly recommended as a base for bath oils. Try adding herb such as mint for an especially invigorating bath. Bottom Rose petals strewn in the bath may look very attractive but the romance wears off when you try to remove them afterwards. A much simpler means of adding herbs to your bath water is to make a bath bag. A 20cm (8in) square of cheesecloth or muslin filled with herbs and then firmly tied with ribbon or string will provide an instant and simple means of infusion.

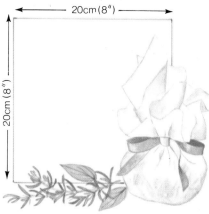

20cm (8″)

20cm (8″)

HERBS IN THE KITCHEN

For centuries herbs have played a vital role in the kitchen, helping to preserve food and making it more palatable and digestible. They were cultivated in the ancient civilizations of Assyria and Babylon, fed by the Egyptians to their slaves, and the Romans added them to practically everything they cooked. Nowadays the use of herbs is equally important to help counter the blandness of modern convenience food and to allow room for expression in terms of individuality and skill in preparing food.

Fresh or dried

It is, of course, preferable to use fresh herbs in cooking, but where this is impossible, dried or frozen ones can be substituted. Remember that the flavour of herbs tends to become more concentrated with drying (although not with freezing) so you need a much smaller amount of them, usually a third to half the amount you would use fresh is sufficient.

If you are forced to rely mainly on dried herbs, try at least to grow or buy fresh parsley. This invaluable fresh-tasting herb is a great help in bringing out the flavour of all dried herbs.

When to add

Some herbs should be added at the beginning of a recipe and others only at the last minute, as prolonged cooking destroys their flavour. Usually a good recipe will tell you when to add seasoning but a rough guide is to add herbs to meat loaves, stuffings, roasts, stocks, soups and casseroles at the beginning of cooking, and to cooked vegetables and sauces ten minutes before the end of cooking time. Uncooked sauces, such as salad dressings will benefit if the herbs are added and left for several hours before use.

It is interesting that flavourings cooked with a dish do tend to become more intense after freezing. So these dishes should either be eaten within two months of preparation, or the herbs omitted at the cooking stage and only added when reheating.

What goes with what

There are no hard and fast rules to this, and once you are used to cooking with herbs you may like to experiment. But for the inexperienced we have included a guide.

Foods/herbs to use with them

Soups
Basil, bay, chervil, chives, coriander, dill, lovage, marjoram, parsley, sage, savory, sweet cicely, tarragon, thyme.

Breads
Basil, coriander, dill, fennel, marjoram, parsley, savory, thyme.

Fish
Basil, bay, dill, lemon balm, lovage, marjoram, rosemary, sage, savory, tarragon, thyme.

Eggs
Basil, bay, chervil, chives, dill, fennel, garlic, marjoram, parsley, rosemary, savory, tarragon, thyme.

Shellfish
Basil, bay, dill, lemon balm, marjoram, savory, tarragon, thyme.

Poultry
Basil, bay, dill, lemon balm, lovage, marjoram, parsley, rosemary, sage, savory, tarragon, thyme.

Lamb
Basil, bay, dill, garlic, marjoram, mint, rosemary, sage, savory, thyme.

However tempting and attractive glass storage jars may look, they are not really suitable containers for herbs. In order to preserve their flavour for as long as possible herbs should be stored in air-tight containers, which do not expose them to the light, and kept in a cool place.

Beef
Basil, bay, chervil, dill, garlic, marjoram, parsley, rosemary, sage, savory, tarragon, thyme.

Pork
Basil, coriander, dill, fennel, marjoram, rosemary, sage, tarragon, thyme.

Vegetables
Basil, bay, chervil, coriander, dandelion, dill, lovage, marjoram, mint, parsley, rosemary, sage, savory, sweet cicely, salad burnet, thyme.

Desserts
Bay, coriander, marigold, thyme, sweet cicely, lemon verbena.

Bouquet garni

Bouquet garni is an essential ingredient in stocks and many soups and casseroles. The classic bouquet garni is made up of a sprig of fresh or dried thyme, a dried bay leaf and a few sprigs of fresh parsley. Tie them up with white thread or string and leave a long end coming out of the pan (tie it to the handle if you like as it often falls in). This enables you to extract the herbs easily before serving—otherwise an unsuspecting guest may get an unpleasant shock. If you are using dried herbs, use one teaspoon and one whole dried bay leaf. Try to avoid using dried parsley, as the flavour is much inferior to that of the fresh herb. These can then be crumbled into a 23cm (8in) circle of muslin or cheesecloth, tightly secured to form a little bag with a long piece of thread or string, and used in the same way as a fresh bouquet garni.

You can vary the herbs in a bouquet garni to suit the ingredients of the particular dish you are preparing. Do not be tempted to add too many different herbs or their flavours will simply cancel each other out. A sprig of rosemary is a good addition to mutton and lamb dishes, tarragon with chicken, marjoram and perhaps a few juniper berries with game, balm or lemon verbena with chicken or fish, and fennel with fish.

Fines herbes
Fines herbes is the French culinary term for a finely chopped fresh herb mixture, usually consisting of parsley, chervil, tarragon and chives. Fines herbes are used as a flavouring for soups, sauces, omelettes and grilled (broiled) meats. As neither chives nor chervil dry very well, try to use fresh or frozen herbs.

Used imaginatively and with discretion herbs can add a new dimension to your cooking. The recipes included in this book are here as a guideline, but with experience and confidence you will soon learn which herb and how much to add, to give your dishes flavour and character.

Top Parsley has numerous culinary uses and may be added to almost all savoury dishes. Although it is easy to freeze parsley does not dry well. The best solution is to grow enough fresh parsley to last the whole year through. *Above* Balm leaves are chiefly used in tisanes but may also be added to fish or lamb dishes. *Left* A basic bouquet garni consists of a few sprigs of fresh parsley and thyme and a bay leaf tied together. If you are using dried herbs they can be tied up in a piece of cheesecloth. *Opposite page* Crushing garlic in a press is one of the most convenient ways of extracting its flavour.

HERBS TO DRINK

Tisanes

A tisane, or tea, is simply an infusion made by adding boiling water to the leaves or flowers of herbs. In many parts of Europe, herbal teas have been an accepted part of the standard eating habits for years. Indeed, a cup of tisane taken after a rich meal is as common as coffee is in other parts of the world. Unlike tea and coffee, however, tisanes contain neither tannin nor caffeine, both strong stimulants, and are much more suitable for aiding the digestion or promoting sleep.

Prepared tisanes are available from herbal shops, homeopathic pharmacists (drugstores) and health food stores in either sachet form or loose. The ailments they are reputed to help are given here but the cures cannot be vouched for.

If you grow your own herbs, why not make your own tisanes? Tisanes may be made from fresh or dried herbs, and full instructions for drying herbs are given in the chapter on preserving herbs (see page 34). The actual preparation is much the same as making ordinary tea, and like ordinary tea it may be drunk on its own or with the addition of milk, a slice of lemon, honey or sugar.

Method If you are making the tisane in individual tea cups, allow one level tablespoon of fresh herbs per cup or one level teaspoon of dried herbs. Pour on boiling water, cover the cup and leave to infuse for three to five minutes. If you are making it in a teapot, allow however many table- or teaspoons required for each cup, plus one for the pot. Leave to infuse for about five minutes and pour through a strainer into the cups.

For teas made from seeds, these should first be pounded in a mortar, and then follow the same process as for dried herbs.

The most common herbs, together with any generally recognized properties they may have, are listed below:

Herb	Part used	Effect
Angelica	Leaves	Helps headaches and exhaustion.
Balm (*Melissa*)	Leaves	Taken hot or cold, this tea is soothing and relaxing.
Basil	Leaves	Taken hot or cold, this tea helps gastric upsets and colds.
Bergamot	Leaves	Drink alone or mixed with China (non-fermented) tea. Relaxing and sleep-inducing.
Borage	Leaves	Hot or cold, borage tea is an exhilarating tonic and helps catarrh.
Catnip	Leaves	A tonic which lessens fever and headaches.
Chamomile	Flowers	Digestive and soothing, particularly useful for sore throats when it may be also used as a gargle.
Coltsfoot	Flowers or leaves	Used for catarrh and chest complaints. Contains vitamin C.
Comfrey	Leaves and dried roots	Soothing and a digestive, helps chest complaints
Dandelion	Leaves	Beneficial to liver, helps rheumatism and acts as a general tonic and blood purifier.
	Roots, dried, roasted and ground	Used as a substitute for coffee, and as a diuretic.

Elder	Flowers	Delicious, sleep-inducing and good for throat infections and colds.
Horehound	Leaves	Coughs and colds.
Hyssop	Leaves	Taken hot or cold helps coughs and colds.
Juniper	Berries	Antiseptic and stimulant, good for chest complaints, indigestion and nerves.
Lady's mantle	Leaves	Premenstrual and menstrual tension.
Lime	Flowers	Delicious, sleep-inducing, soothing drink, good for colds and indigestion.
Lovage	Leaves	More like a broth, add salt for a cleansing and refreshing drink.
Melilot	Whole plant	Wind and general tonic.
Mint (*especially peppermint and spearmint*)	Leaves	Taken for colds, headaches, diarrhea, heartburn, nausea and stomachache.
Nettle	Leaves	General tonic and blood purifier.
Parsley	Leaves	General tonic and diuretic. Helps rheumatism.
Rosemary	Leaves	Headaches and insomnia.
Sage	Leaves	General tonic.
Thyme	Leaves	Good for coughs and sinus ailments.
Vervain (*verbena*)	Leaves and dried roots	Slightly bitter tisane, acts as a sedative and digestive.
Yarrow	Leaves	Taken for fevers, coughs, colds and as a general tonic.

Tisanes may also be made from the seeds of fennel and caraway and the leaves of tansy, costmary and St. John's wort.

Do not expect instant results from drinking a tisane, their benefits are cumulative.

Herbal beer and wine

Wine and beer have been made in the home since time immemorial and, as commercial wines become more and more expensive, interest in this ancient domestic art is reviving. Almost any fruit, vegetable or herb can be used for wine making and brewing beer—even the dregs of tea.

A number of shops sell very adequate wine making kits and equipment. Once the initial outlay has been made it is only necessary to purchase the ingredients for subsequent batches as the equipment can be used over and over again.

Herb beer

Herbal beer is a term usually applied to beers made with herbs other than hops. The hop is, however, a wild herb as well as being widely cultivated for beer making.

After the initial investment in equipment, the cost of making beer, especially from herbs like the common nettle, is relatively small.

Equipment
Large pan (sufficient to contain all the weeds collected)
4.5 litre/1 gallon (10 pint) polythene or plastic fermenting vessel with a lid (a polythene or plastic bucket will suffice)
Strainer or remnant of terylene net curtain
Wooden spoons

Above *The flowers of the elder are used to make a tisane which tastes slightly of muscatel. As well as having an attractive taste, an elderflower tea promotes sleep and helps alleviate sore throats.* Opposite page *Long before the hop, a wild herb which can also be cultivated, was used in brewing, beer tended to be cereal-based. Some beers still rely on barley as a principal ingredient. Beer was commonly drunk up until the introduction of tea, and every housewife would have had to brew a regular supply for her family.*

Bucket or other larger container
Beer bottles (cleaned and sterilized) and stoppers

The equipment should always be used spotlessly clean and if possible sterilised. (Kits for sterilising babies' bottles are useful for this.)

Nettle beer

Using rubber gloves and scissors gather fresh, young green stinging nettle shoots. Take only the top two or three pairs of leaves. The quantity is not vital, but the shoots, not pressed down, should just about fill the brewing bucket. This will make approximately 4.5 litres/1 gallon (10 pints).

Crystal malt, hops and ale yeast (for quantity follow the manufacturer's instructions) are obtainable from home wine and beer kit suppliers. One teaspoon of citric acid may be substituted for the juice of half a lemon.

	Metric/U.K.	U.S.
Nettles		
Crystal malt (broken)	125g/4oz	4oz
Malt extract	1kg/2lb	2lb
Sugar	250g/8oz	1 cup
1 handful of dried hops		
Juice of ½ lemon		
Salt	¼ tsp	¼ tsp
Yeast		

Simmer the washed nettles and crystal malt in a large pan for about 40 minutes.

Put malt extract, sugar, lemon juice and salt into the fermenting vessel fitted with a good lid and strain contents on to the washed nettles and crystal malt. A remnant of terylene net curtain is preferable to an open strainer. The nettle shoots should be squeezed by gloved hands, to extract the full flavour. Stir the mixture thoroughly.

Make the quantity up to 4.5 litres/1 gallon (10 pints) with tap water.

When cool (between 18°-20°C or 65°-70°F), stir in yeast according to the manufacturer's instructions. Maintain this temperature, and keep the vessel covered.

Allow to ferment for four to seven days. Remove the yeast from the top at intervals if necessary. When fermentation has finished the liquid looks clear and bubbles cease to rise. Siphon beer into another clean container.

Dissolve 50g/2oz (¼ cup) sugar in a small quantity of hot water. Add to the beer. Siphon into clean beer bottles and stopper down well. Store in a warm room for two days.

Transfer to a cool place and store for at least a month before drinking.

Herb wine

Herbal wines are made from an infusion of the chosen herb often referred to as herb tea or tisane. The spent herbs must be strained out of the infusion. A remnant of net curtain or muslin can be made into a bag and and the herbs placed in this. The bag is then pressed to extract the full flavour.

The most welcome modern adjunct to home wine making is concentrated pure grape juice. Old recipes for herbal wines usually add dried grapes, often picturesquely described as 'raisins of the sun'. Grape concentrate is a trouble free substitute and gives excellent vinosity. The variety available is enormous.

The mixture of liquids to be fermented is called the must.

Yeast Fermentation is caused by the addition of yeast to the must. If you have been browsing through old books you will be familiar with the recommendation to float brewer's yeast on toast in the liquid—this should be avoided at all costs. A vigorous fermentation can be obtained using

Ingredients and equipment, including a corking-tool, used for wine making. Many of these items will already be in the home while the others are inexpensive to buy and will quickly repay the small initial outlay.

dried baker's yeast, but it is preferable to use a true wine yeast (available from home wine kit suppliers). There are several quick-acting, general purpose yeasts which produce reliable results. To work effectively, the yeast needs sustaining by the addition of certain salts. These are bought ready mixed as yeast nutrient (available from home wine kit suppliers). Use more or less nutrient in relation to the quantity of fruit juice you use. Follow the manufacturer's instructions as these will vary.

Yeast works best in an acid medium. Herb infusions may be low in acid. By adding the juice of lemons or oranges or crystals of citric acid this can be remedied.

Sweetener Honey was the traditional sweetener of the herbal wine maker. In wines made with bitter herbs the dual taste of the sharp leaf or flower and the soft sweetness of honey is a gastronomic delight. Whenever you can—use honey in place of sugar to sweeten your wine. The wine is then called a melomel.

Equipment The basic equipment needed for home wine making is extremely simple and costs very little. Some of the items may already be in the home.

9 litre/2 gallon (20 pint) boiling container
9 litre/2 gallon (20 pint) plastic pail with a lid
4.5 litre/1 gallon (10 pint) fermentation and storage jars
Airlock for each fermentation jar
Plain bungs to fit the fermentation jars for storage
A siphon tube at least 1.2m/4ft long
Wine bottles
Corks
Corking tool
Nylon strainer—at least 15cm/6in in diameter
Funnel—at least 15cm/6in diameter

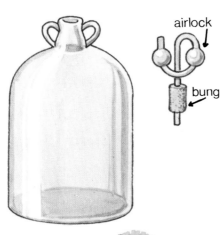

airlock

bung

calyx

Top *Two pieces of equipment used in making wine: a fermentation jar and an air-lock with bung.* Above *Dandelion wine has an attractive and interesting flavour. Pick the dandelions on a sunny day, shake out any insects and twist off the calyx and stems as these impart a bitter flavour.*

Do not use any equipment made of iron, steel, copper and brass as these will spoil your wine. In all wine making it is essential to keep equipment clean and sterile. The method for all the recipes given here is basically the same.

Dandelion wine

Pick the dandelion flowers on a warm, sunny morning. Shake out any small insects. Then holding the yellow petals with one hand, twist off the calyx and stem. These are too bitter for wine and should be discarded.

	Metric/U.K.	U.S.
Dandelion petals	1.2L/2pt	5 cups
*Commerical grape concentrate	½ can	½ can
Lemon	1	1
Orange	1	1
Citric acid	1 tsp	1 tsp
Infused tea or	175ml/6floz	¾ cup
grape tannin	¼ tsp	¼ tsp
Sugar or clear honey	700g/1½lb	3 cups
Wine yeast and nutrient		
Campden tablets		

*Can grape concentrate refers to the size sold to make 4½L/1 gallon (10 pints) of wine.

Place everything except the dandelions and the yeast into a bucket. Make an infusion of the dandelion flowers and allow to stand for about half an hour. Strain the infusion into the bucket and stir thoroughly until all is dissolved. Allow to cool to 24°C (75°F) and add yeast.

Fermentation The bucket should be placed in a warm room for the first fermentation which should last from three to six days. This is the aerobic (in the presence of air) fermentation, nevertheless the bucket must have a lid or be fitted with a clean cloth held in place by a firm band.

As the yeast starts to work considerable bubbling and frothing cocurs. The must will change to a milky colour as the yeast grows.

Once the fermentation gets under way the must should be transferred to a fermentation jar. This should be topped up with water and a fermentation or air lock fixed.

Keep an eye on the fermentation lock for the first few days to make sure there is always water present to maintain the trap. Evaporation may necessitate topping up daily. The temperature should be maintained at about 21°C (70°F).

Fermentation will gradually decrease and after about four or five weeks the line of bubbles around the top of the container will have died completely away—if not wait another few days to make sure no gas is being given off.

Storage Dead yeast and perhaps other solid matter (the lees) will by now have settled at the bottom of the fermentation jar. If left there unpleasant flavour may be imparted to the wine, so they should be removed.

To do this the wine has to be siphoned into a second sterilized container with a siphon tube. Stand the wine container on a table and set the second container on the floor. This process is called racking the wine and must be done several times.

The lower container should be topped up with cooled boiled water if necessary as it is preferable to have the minimum of air space remaining.

Crush one campden tablet per 4.5 litre/1 gallon (10 pints) of wine and add before sealing the container with a solid bung or safety lock—these tablets act as a preservative and help to stop further fermentation. Store in a cool dry place.

Above *Wine can be made from many flowers other than those of the dandelion. Rose petals in particular make a delightfully fragant wine.* Left *A selection of home-made wines will enrich and enlarge your wine cellar.*

Rack off the wine into a clean container every eight weeks or so, to remove sediment till the wine becomes clearer.

Bottling When the wine is clear, then only is it ready to be bottled. For each 4.5 litres/1 gallon (10 pints) wine you will need six sterilized bottles and corks. Always label your bottles. The wine should then be stored from three to six months although, like herb beer, it will improve for keeping a month or so longer if possible.

Many flowers can be used instead of dandelions. Broom, clover, coltsfoot, cowslip and roses all make delightful wine.

Some flowers such as the carnation, elderflower, chamomile and wall-flower have a more pungent taste and should be used sparingly. No more than 0.5 litre/1 pint (2½ cups) flowers should be infused for each 4.5 litres/1 gallon (10 pints) wine.

Any herb which makes a herb tea or tisane can be used as a basis for wine. Lemon balm, sage, rosemary, raspberry leaves, borage and comfrey are recommended. Young blackberry shoots also make a light wine. There is always lots of room for experimentation.

HERBS TO PRESERVE

There is nothing quite like the flavour and aroma of fresh herbs, but as many are annuals and not available throughout the whole year, the answer is to preserve them in the way most appropriate to their use.

Harvesting

The art of harvesting and preserving herbs to retain as much of their essential qualities as possible, is one that is acquired with practice. There are, however, a few simple rules, which if followed should produce successful results:

Always gather herbs in the early morning, after the dew has had time to dry and before the sun has drawn out and dispersed their volatile oils.

Do not pick herbs when they are damp after rain.

Cut them with a sharp knife, except for chives which should be cut with scissors.

Place the cut herbs in one layer in a tray or shallow box.

Never collect more than you can deal with immediately. Herbs left lying around quickly deteriorate and lose their essential oils.

Keep different herbs separate from one another, to avoid cross-flavouring.

Handle as little as possible to avoid bruising.

Leaves Pick in the summer time, just before flowering when their volatile oils are at their peak. Leave the leaves attached to the stem. Discard any leaves which are not perfect.

Flowers Pick as soon as they are fully open, and only select those which are absolutely unblemished. Lavender, wormwood, southernwood, roses, hyssop, chamomile and bergamot are all suitable.

Berries Gather when they are fully ripe, glossy and well coloured but before they darken or stiffen.

Seeds Cut the stems with seed heads on of lovage, dill, fennel and coriander for example, as soon as the seeds are ready to fall and the seed heads have turned brown.

Roots Gather in the autumn, except for horseradish which may be harvested at any time.

After harvesting, there are several ways to concentrate the oils and aromatic properties of herbs so that you can use them for cooking, making cosmetics and pot-pourri throughout the year.

Drying

All herbs should be dried in an airy, shady place where there is no danger of condensation. There are several methods of drying, choose the one that is most appropriate to your circumstances.

Herbs contain approximately 80% of water. The object of drying them is to remove this water without losing any of their valuable properties. About 3.6kg/8lb of fresh herbs are needed to produce ½kg/1lb of dried herbs.

Your aim is to dry the herbs quite quickly with an even, low warmth—not less than 21°C (70°F) or more than 38°C (100°F). A good, even ventilation is just as important as the heat to carry away the humidity of the drying plants. Too much heat or too sunny or light a place will brown the leaves, or at least, dissipate the aromatic properties you are trying to conserve. So you want a dark place with little or no dust, but warmth and plenty of air.

Possible drying places are an airing cupboard or a clothes drying cupboard; a plate-warming compartment of an oven; a darkened, warm,

Those herbs which do not grow all the year round may be preserved for use when out of season by drying or freezing. One of the oldest methods is by air drying, where bunches of herbs are hung upside down in a dry, airy place until all the superfluous moisture has evaporated.

well-ventilated room, passage or cupboard where you could set up a small fan heater; an attic, garage or darkened green-house, a dry, well-aired cellar, perhaps near a boiler.

The shelves must be well separated so that air can pass freely between them. You could use muslin tacked to a wooden framework, hessian or any open weave cloth stretched over dowels or framing, or the flat bottoms of cardboard boxes which have been perforated to let air through, but do not use wire mesh.

If you can alter and regulate the heat, one method is to begin drying with a temperature of about 32 °C (90 °F) for one day and then reduce the heat to 21 °C (70 °F) until the drying process is finished.

The drying space should only faintly smell of herbs; a strong smell means there is too much heat and escaping aromas. Don't add a fresh batch of herbs until the first batch is dry or you will add more humidity to the air. Turn the herbs as they are drying from time to time.

Air drying Tying a bunch of herbs and flowers and hanging them upside down in a dry, airy space is an old method of drying herbs, and more satisfactory in a dry climate than in a humid one. Air drying is likely to retain less colour and scent but needs no special arrangements.

Experiment with drying until you get the fullest colour and smell in the herbs. It takes from four to fourteen days or more to dry herbs and flowers. Some flowers, such as rosemary flowers, are better dried slowly at a lower temperature than herbs.

Leaves are dry when they are brittle but will not shatter. Flower petals should feel dry and slightly crisp. Roots should dry right through with no soft centre. The dried roots should then be ground like coffee beans. Seeds should be dried for a few hours in the sun after they have been removed from the seed heads.

Storing Strip leaves from their stems, crumble them—but not too finely or they will quickly lose their flavour—and put them into clean, air-tight containers and store in a cool, dark place. Some herbs, such as sage, thyme and rosemary can be left on the stalk. (This makes them easier to put into casseroles and stews and remove afterwards when the cooking is completed.) Dried bay leaves should be kept whole. Seeds and flower heads should be put straight into an air-tight container.

If moisture starts to form on the inside of the container, the herbs have not been dried correctly. Put them on to paper and allow a further drying time.

Dried herbs in general last a year at the most, and the more finely powdered they are the sooner they lost their taste. It is a good idea to date your containers so that you know exactly how long you have had the herbs. Lemon balm, parsley, summer savory and tarragon only last nine months to a year when dried. Basil, lovage, mint and marjoram last a year or more. And rosemary, sage and thyme can last longer still—but it is a good idea to replace them yearly if you can.

Freezing

Freezing is one of the best methods of preserving herbs for culinary use as the flavour, appearance, texture and nutritional value remain virtually unchanged. It is particularly suitable for soft-leaved herbs which do not dry quite so well, such as mint, chives, parsley, balm, fennel, basil, dill and sorrel. Always freeze herbs in small quantities and remember that while they are perfectly good for cooking, they are not suitable for garnishes.

Having harvested your herbs, wash them if they are not clean and shake dry. If you intend to use them within two months they can be frozen as they are. For longer storage tie them in bunches, dip each bunch first in boiling water and then in chilled water to blanch them. Either leave the herbs whole but separate them into small bunches, or chop them up

Below Thyme, *including lemon* thyme *illustrated here, responds well to drying and will last for a year or more without losing its flavour. Bottom* Balm *also dries well but should not really be used dried after about nine months. It is a good idea to replace dried herbs annually if you can.*

Tarragon makes a particularly good salad oil and enables you to enjoy the flavour of this herb throughout the year.

finely with a sharp knife or a pair of scissors. Whole herbs, or bouquets garnis, may be packed in foil or plastic bags, sealed and frozen. Chopped herbs should be packed tightly into an ice-cube tray and topped up with water and frozen. When the cubes are solid turn them out into a plastic bag. In both cases make sure the wrapping has been previously labelled. Bouquet garni and whole sprigs may be used straight from the freezer. If you wish to chop whole leaves, this can be done by simply crumbling the leaf while it is still frozen. Chopped herbs in cubes may also be added to dishes straight from the freezer, or if you prefer, the cubes of chopped leaves may be left to thaw in a fine strainer.

Herbs have a freezer life of about six months.

Herbal oils

Herbal oils are a boon in the kitchen if you want to marinate, brown meats and braise, baste, make fried rice, cook in oil and make salad dressings. They can also be used, made in a slightly different way, in beauty preparations (see page 16).

Herbs that make good culinary oils are basil, savory, fennel, thyme, rosemary and tarragon. The taste of basil goes well with tomatoes, so cook ratatouille in basil oil; fennel goes well with fish and in salads; tarragon suits fish, poultry or meats; thyme is excellent with vegetables.

If possible make your herb oils in summer as strong sunlight is needed for the aromatic oils to be extracted from the herbs.

Method Crush the freshly cut herbs in a pestle and mortar, or put them through a blender. Put two tablespoons of the pounded herbs in a 300ml/ $\frac{1}{2}$ pint ($1\frac{1}{4}$ cups) crock or wide-necked, screw-top bottle. Fill three-quarters full with sunflower, corn, vegetable or olive oil. Add one tablespoon of wine vinegar and three or four black peppercorns. Seal the bottle tightly and put it somewhere where it will receive hot sunlight. Leave it for two to three weeks, shaking the bottle once or twice a day. After this time, strain off the oil, pressing all the oil out of the crushed herbs and discard the herbs.

Repeat the process with freshly cut herbs for another three weeks. Then test to see if the oil is sufficiently saturated. A little oil on the back of the hand should really smell of the herb.

If there is not enough sunshine to bring out the flavour of the herb then you can put the crock or bottle, securely fastened of course, into a double boiler and warm it below boiling point for a few hours each day. The oil should be strong enough after seven or eight days of this treatment.

When the oil is ready, pour it through a strainer set over a funnel into a dry clean bottle. Add a sprig of the fresh herbs for decoration, tightly cork the bottle and store for use as required.

Herbal vinegars

Vinegar, like alcohol, is another good medium for absorbing the flavour and aromatic qualities of herbs. They will improve any salad dressing or marinade, particularly in winter when many fresh herbs are unobtainable. Like herbal oils they may be used as a bath additive. (See page 22).

Excellent vinegars can be made using the leaves of one or more of the following herbs: lemon balm, basil, borage, salad burnet, dill, fennel, marjoram, summer savory, mint, tarragon (tarragon vinegar can also be bought) and thyme. Or try mixing some of them—such as summer savory, marjoram, chives and tarragon.

Use only fresh herbs gathered according to the harvesting instructions at the beginning of this chapter. You will need about 125g/4oz (2 cups) of leaves to 1.2 litre/1 quart (5 cups) of vinegar.

You can use red or white wine vinegar, cider vinegar or malt vinegar. White wine vinegar goes well with tarragon, basil and salad burnet; cider vinegar suits mint, and red wine vinegar goes well with garlic.

Herbs add their own special flavours to cooking and salad oils and vinegar. They can be made simply by steeping the herb in oil. From left to right: thyme oil, rosemary oil and dill vinegar.

Wash and dry the leaves and pack loosely into a wide-mouthed glass jar. Pour over the vinegar and add two or three black peppercorns. Cover the jar tightly and put it where you will remember to shake it, or stir the contents with a wooden spoon, every other day.

After ten days taste it. If it is not herby enough strain out the herb leaves and discard them. Add fresh leaves and start all over again. Leave for another ten days and check again.

When the vinegar is flavoured enough, strain it into bottles through a funnel. Push in a sprig of fresh herb for decoration and cork or cap tightly.

Vinegar from seeds Herbal vinegars from coriander or dill seeds have a spicy flavour—dill tastes mildly of caraway. Bruise the seeds with a pestle and mortar. Allow two tablespoons of seeds to every 1.2 litre/1 quart (5 cups) of vinegar. Put them into a jar and pour over warmed vinegar. Cork or cover the jar tightly and put in a warm place for two weeks, shaking it from time to time. When the vinegar is ready. strain it into clean dry bottles through a funnel lined with filter paper, muslin or cheesecloth and cork tightly.

Garlic vinegar Put garlic cloves into vinegar. Leave for twenty-four hours and then remove them.

HERBS FOR EVER

The fragrance of sweet smelling herbs, spices and flowers can be captured all the year round in pot-pourri and sachets. Rooms, closets, household and personal linen can be kept fragrant and fresh with aromatic plants. You can give each drawer, closet or cupboard a distinctive scent—sweet, spicy, delicate or intoxicating—making it both a special pleasure to open it and the contents delightful to wear or use.

Herbs and flowers grow everywhere. They can be gathered and dried at home (as explained on page 34) or bought already dried at herb shops and mixed at home with essential oils and fixatives to make their scents last. It is in the subtle blending of these fragrances, and in the use of colour, that the art of making pot-pourri and herb mixtures for sachets lies.

Pot pourri

The making of pot-pourri is an old but still popular method of presenting dried flowers and leaves so that their perfume may continue to be enjoyed. Indeed, they can be made from all scented plants—flowers, fruits, herbs, barks, spices—and it is the combination of these that produces the dimly fragrant, sometimes mysterious aromas.

Each pot-pourri should have a main scent, or base, usually of rose petals to which the other ingredients are added. Obviously it is best to choose a rose which is highly scented, such as a damask rose. The dried petals should be placed in an air-tight container, and for every large handful of rose petals, a small handful of salt should be added.

Leave the salted petals for about a week, shaking or stirring them once or twice a day. Once you have a base scent, the other leaves and flowers may be added. Choose from dried flowers such as pinks, carnations, honeysuckle, orange blossom, jasmine, lavender, sweet peas, chamomile, elder, marigolds, nasturtiums, mignonette, heliotrope, lime flowers, violets, wallflowers, jonquils, lily of the valley, acacia, oleander and gardenias. Other flowers which may be added for visual effect, although they do not retain their scent, are borage and pansies.

Leaves could include those of angelica, bergamot, verbena, lovage, lavender, southernwood, bay, myrtle, sage, sweet cicely, tarragon, eucalyptus, basil, sweet marjoram, lemon and orange thyme, balm, mint and rosemary, while spices, such as cloves, nutmeg, coriander, cinnamon, mace, vanilla pod, woodruff, sandalwood and cedar also make attractive additions. Thinly pared orange and lemon peel which has been dried in a cool oven, warming drawer or any closed dry space, and then pounded in a mortar or ground, add scent and colour.

To whatever combination of ingredients you choose you can then add a few drops of essential oils, bought from a herb shop, to reinforce a particular fragrance. Finally a fixative, such as powdered orris root, is needed to hold the perfume longer than the flowers would naturally.

Opposite page *Making a pot-pourri enables you to capture the sweet fresh scents of summer all the year. Simple to prepare they also make marvellous presents. Numerous recipes for pot-pourri have been handed down to successive generations, but why not experiment with your own mixtures? Below Once you have made your selections of flowers and leaves for pot-pourri, you need a fixative to hold the perfume. The seed of the coriander plant is one of the ingredients in the fixative recipe given in this chapter.*

Fixative

	Metric/U.K.	U.S.
Oil of lavender	30ml/1floz	2 Tbs
Orris root	125g/4oz	4oz
Ground mace	25g/1oz	2 Tbs
Cloves	25g/1oz	2 Tbs
Coriander seed	25g/1oz	2 Tbs

Mix the oil into the ground orris root, and when they are thoroughly combined, add the remaining ingredients. Stir the mixture into the rose petals, cover and leave for a month, stirring occasionally. If the mixture is too dry and powdery, add more flower petals. If the mixture is too moist, add more orris root. Finally pour the pot-pourri into a suitable container and it is ready for use.

The combinations of colour and scent are endless but there are a few recipes you may like to try. The fluid measurement refers to the amount of space the petals take up in a measuring jug or cup.

Floral pot-pourri

	Metric/U.K.	U.S.
Rose petals	1L/2pt	5 cups
Rose geranium leaves	½L/1pt	2½ cups
Lavender flowers	½L/1pt	2½ cups
Rosemary leaves	225ml/8floz	1 cup
FIXATIVE		
Ground cloves	2 Tbs	2 Tbs
Ground cinnamon	2 Tbs	2 Tbs
Grated nutmeg	2 Tbs	2 Tbs
Ground orris root	3 Tbs	3 Tbs
Ground gum benzoin	3 Tbs	3 Tbs
Oil of rose	20 drops	20 drops
Oil of sandalwood	5 drops	5 drops

Jasmine pot-pourri

	Metric/U.K.	U.S.
Jasmine flowers	½L/1pt	2½ cups
Orange blossoms	125ml/4floz	½ cup
Gardenias	125ml/4floz	½ cup
Lemon- and rose-scented geranium leaves	225ml/8floz	1 cup
FIXATIVE		
Cassia	50g/2oz	4 Tbs
Ground gum benzoin	50g/2oz	4 Tbs
Oil of vanilla	20 drops	20 drops

Pomanders can be used to scent closets, cupboards and drawers and make very attractive presents. You can make your own pomander, simply and inexpensively, by following the instructions on the opposite page.

Containers If you are making a beautifully scented pot-pourri, the presentation is also important. Choose an attractive apothecary jar, cermic pot, china or porcelain, box or urn, and add flowers for colour rather than scent, such as borage. Pot-pourris are not only lovely to have in your own home, they make delightful and welcome presents.

Pomanders

Pomanders were originally mixtures of aromatic herbs and spices carried around in perforated boxes or spheres of gold, silver or ivory to ward off infection and the unpleasant smells that were prevalent before the days of barns and sewerage.

The word pomander is derived from the old French *pomme d'ambre*, or apple of amber. Amber probably refers to ambergris which was used as a perfume base, although it was also the name for a medieval alloy of four parts gold to one part silver.

By the late Middle Ages, the containers were elaborately chased and decorated and hung from lovely chains. It was thought in medieval and Tudor times that plague was in the air and carried on the prevailing wind—so it made sense to sniff your own private disinfectant mixture.

China pomanders Perforated china pomanders are now available in large stores and gift shops. Some of the ingredients in old pomander mixtures included cassia, cinnamon, cloves, benzoin, betel nuts, musk, frankincense and bay leaves. You can try these too and also use many other herbs and flowers (or essential oils of flowers), woods or citrus fruits to make your own old-fashioned pomander.

Another version of a pomander was a scooped out orange shell filled with spices, or an orange stuck with cloves and rolled in spices. Old orange and clove pomanders still in existence are shrunk to tiny proportions and iron-hard—for the fruit dries out and shrivels but doesn't rot. You can make your own pomander, simply and inexpensively, to scent closets, cupboards and drawers, and act as a moth deterrent or to give as delightful and unusual presents. Try hanging a few on your Christmas tree, they not only look pretty, but the mixture of scents—orange, cinnamon and pine—is delicious.

Method 1

	Metric/U.K.	U.S.
Large, fresh, thin-skinned orange	1	1
One jar of whole cloves		
Ground cinnamon	2 tsp	2 tsp
Orris root powder	2 tsp	2 tsp

Make a ring of holes around the middle of the orange with a toothpick, wooden skewer, or cocktail stick; and press a whole clove into each hole, or work directly, simply pressing in cloves working in circles towards each end. The cloves should be so close together that the entire orange skin is covered.

Mix together the cinnamon and orris root powder. Roll the clove-studded orange thoroughly in the mixture so that as much of it is taken up as possible. Wrap in tissue paper and put in a dark, dry drawer for three to five weeks. During this time the orange will dry through completely and shrink slightly.

Take the orange out and shake off any surplus powder. The pomander is now ready for use.

Orris root Orris root powder is the ground, dried root of a variety of iris *Iris florentina*. The powder does have a delicate perfume but its chief purpose is as a fixative for the other scents. It is available from herb shops but can be omitted without ill effect.

To make a be-ribboned pomander

It is possible simply to tie ribbon around the orange leaving a loop at the top for hanging, or to insert a loop of ribbon through a staple pressed into the top of the orange. For a smoother effect, however, leave two channels in the orange, wide enough to lay a ribbon in, when you are sticking in the cloves. This way the cloved pomander will be dried into four sections, as shown in fig. 1a.

When you have completed studding the orange and left it to dry out, cut one piece of ribbon long enough to go around the circumference of the orange, and pin the ends together at the top with dressmaking pins. Cut a second piece of ribbon, that measures the circumference of the orange plus enough to make a bow or a loop with which to hang up the pomander (fig. 1b) and tie it to the pomander, fitting the ribbon around the remaining channel.

Use velvet ribbon in old-fashioned shades of soft pink, crimson, or braid two or three ribbons together.

Floral pomander In addition to cloves, you can also use fresh flowers to decorate the pomander, such as rosebuds, jasmine or sprigs of lavender.

It is reassuring to note that the orange will not rot but become petrified and shrink slightly. The fragrance lasts for several years, and although we cannot pretend that it will protect you from infections, we are sure that it will give you pleasure.

Fig 1a: *To make a be-ribboned pomander, two channels, wide enough to lay a ribbon in, should be left when you are sticking in the cloves. Fig 1b. When the orange is completely studded, cut one piece of ribbon the same length as the circumference of the orange, attach and fasten with pins. Cut a second length long enough to make a bow or loop with which to hang it, and tie it around the remaining channel.*

Fig 1a

Fig 1b

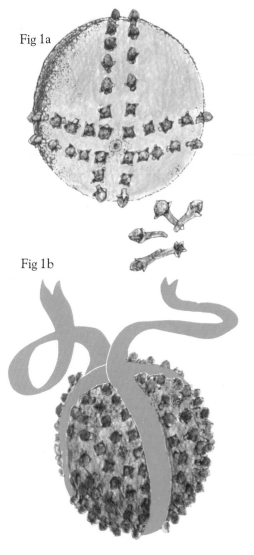

Herb pillows

For dreams of summer why not slip a herb pillow into your pillowcase? Herb pillows have been used since Victorian days to soothe the nerves and to induce a refreshing sleep. Indeed, the clean, fresh scent of a little lavender cushion tucked behind the head was held to be an excellent cure for the vapours.

The simplest way to provide yourself with a herb pillow is to make a bag of whatever size you require out of cotton, linen, cheesecloth or muslin, to hold the herbs. Then make a cover for it that can be laundered in sprigged cotton, or white embroidery on white cotton, or perhaps in gay, bold stripes or other patterns. Then fill the inside bag with soporific and sweet-smelling *dried* herbs from the following collection of mixtures.

Mixture 1 Use equal quantities of lavender, lemon verbena and peppermint for an aromatic base. In addition, for sleep-inducing properties, add small quantities of any of the following herbs—all of which are pleasantly scented and will blend well together: angelica, bergamot, dill, hops, balm, marjoram, rosemary, sage or thyme.

Mixture 2 Mix together equal parts of rosemary blossoms, rosemary leaves, pine needles, rose geranium leaves and balm.

Mixture 3 Mix together equal parts of rose petals and lavender, and add small amounts of woodruff, chamomile, dill, sage, bergamot and tarragon.

Mixture 4 Use hops only. Many people feel a hops pillow is best for insomnia.

Herb sachets

Smaller bags, enclosing the same herbs as those used in herbal pillows, not only scent cupboards and drawers but also act as moth deterrents. The addition of a dried stalk or two of southernwood or wormwood is particularly good for repelling moths as well as giving a subtle aromatic scent. It is interesting to note that the French name for southernwood is *garderobe*.

Sachets can be made of small squares of silk, printed cotton or organdie, and treated as miniature pillows, or they can be gathered across the top and secured with a ribbon. This method means that they can be refilled later on. Fill either with mixtures of herbs as suggested for pillows, or simply one herb, such as lemon verbena or lavender, or try some of the following mixtures.

Mixture 1 Equal quantities of tansy, rosemary and southernwood or wormwood plus 15g/½oz of ground cloves. This is both sweet-scented and moth repelling.

Mixture 2 Equal quantities of santolina (cotton lavender, or santonica), wormwood, mint and tansy plus a crushed cinnamon stick. Mix well and add a little dried lemon or orange peel. This mixture also acts as an insect repellent.

Mixture 3 Equal quantities of southernwood or wormwood and balm, with twice the amount of rose petals, and twice as much again of lavender. A few crushed coriander seeds, cloves or cinnamon can be added.

Lavender bags

This pretty selection of lavender cushions has a general theme in terms of colour but variety is achieved with the use of different, lightweight fabrics.

Each completed cushion measures about 7cm (3in) square, except for the gathered-up sachets, which are rectangular in shape. (If you choose a fabric with an open weave you will also need lining fabric.) Cut out a back and front from the fabric, with a small seam allowance on each side. Embroider fabric with cross stitch, satin stitch, leaf or running stitch in contrasting threads. Alternatively, sew on trimmings such as lace or rickrack.

With right sides facing, sew the two pieces together leaving one side open. Turn sachet right side out and fill with lavender. Whip stitch open side seams together.

Note that the gathered-up sachets have been back stitched; in one example a frayed edge has been introduced.

For further finishing touches add bows or fabric flowers, as appropriate.

Lavender bags provide an attractive way of scenting your clothes and linen. Small pieces of fabric left over from making dresses and furnishings are ideal for this purpose.

HERBS FOR GARDENS & POTS

Herbs are pretty, aromatic, useful and above all fun to grow. Nearly all herbs grow best in the open ground, with a few exceptions they also do well in containers and tubs, and most can be grown successfully indoors as well.

Herbs in the garden

There is room in every garden to grow a few herbs. If you do not have enough room to devote one specific area to herbs, they are quite happy to grow among vegetables, fruit and flowers. If you do have more space then a herb garden is a delight. They need not be large, but they should be enclosed, by a wall or hedging, or in a sheltered position and the plants spaced out. Herb gardens are very pleasant to sit in or walk through, occasionally picking a leaf and crushing it to release its perfume. On hot days, the aromatic scent of the herbs will permeate the whole garden.

The idea that herb gardens need be near the kitchen may be ignored. Choose the most suitable place and if you have to change your footwear to pick them this isn't really very serious. It is more important that your garden should look neat and that you are able to reach each plant to pick it with ease. This can be achieved by dividing the garden into squares, in a checkerboard design and separating one herb from the next with squares of stone or brick. Or you may choose to arrange them in the traditional wheel pattern, in which case the spokes could be defined in gravel paths. (A sundial or rose or bay tree in the centre looks very attractive.) Paths of chamomile, creeping thyme or pennyroyal are also attractive and produce a delicious scent when walked on. The design may be bold or formal so long as it is functional as well as decorative.

Divisions between herbs also prevent plants getting mixed up, so if you do not like the idea of stones or bricks you could cultivate small, low-growing hedges of rosemary or lavender. These, however, need regular clipping to keep them neat.

Planning a herb garden Any herb garden, whether it is a simple border or based on the more complicated Elizabethan designs, needs careful thought. You must know about the heights and growing habits of the plants, otherwise your tall subjects may be planted in the front of the bed, or near to and smothering the short or creeping herbs. Similarly, different herbs have different requirements in terms of liking sun or shade, heavy or light soil. All these details are specified individually in the growing section of this book, so only general requirements will be referred to here.

Situation and soil Most herbs come originally from the Mediterranean countries, where they grow in dry, poor and sometimes rocky soil. So unless your climate and soil are similar, choose a sheltered spot facing the sun for your herb garden and make sure that the soil is well-drained. Herbs will usually grow in most soils except for heavy clay. If possible it is a good idea to have the ground sloping slightly towards the south as this helps with drainage. Then herbs that need sun can be planted at the top of the slope, and those that prefer a damper, shadier spot can be put in the bottom.

Which herbs to grow This is, of course, a question of personal taste and the size of the proposed herb garden. Also you may wish to grow them for a specific use, either for cooking, cosmetics, for their scent or for their medicinal use, but a small selection of the better known herbs, both annuals and perennials, will give you a useful stock for cooking. If you wish to attract bees, butterflies and other pollen-collecting insects, then

Opposite page The John Blair Herb Garden in Williamsburg, USA, was designed in 1937 as part of the colonial restoration of this village, which is why it has the simple formality reminiscent of much older, traditional gardens. Below Although rue is now grown principally for its decorative qualities, it was once regarded as being both beneficial to the eyesight and as a protection from plague and jail fever. Sprigs of rue were always included in the small bouquets of flowers, called tussie-mussies, carried by judges in the law courts. Its inclusion was in no way due to its perfume, however, which, to say the least, is unpleasant.

Below *Used as a garnish and flavouring throughout the world, parsley is in constant demand by cooks everywhere. It will grow successfully both indoors and outside and is an attractive as well as a useful herb.*
Centre *Angelica growing in a pretty and informal setting*
Bottom *A traditional herb garden where the plants are decoratively separated by low-growing hedges and brick paths.*

grow flowering herbs such as lavender, thyme, savory, hyssop and bergamot. All such features are mentioned under the individual growing specifications of each herb.

Preparing the soil The better prepared the bed is the better the garden will be. The soil, of whatever type, should be well dug, a certain amount of compost worked in, given a final raking and firmed. Do all this in the early autumn and then give the bed a final dig in the spring prior to planting.

Growing from seed Some herbs, the annuals and those which will self-seed but for the purposes of cultivation are treated as annuals, are freshly grown from seed each spring.

Sow the seeds as soon as the danger of frost is over. (Most seed packets from reputable seed companies have good directions on them.) Water the soil. Sow the seeds thinly—otherwise the seedlings will choke each other as they try to grow—and then press the soil down lightly with a board.

The seeds can be sown where the plants are to grow—*Anthriscus cerefolium* (chervil), for example, hates being moved—and then thinned out to the required distance apart when the seedlings are 5-8cm (2-3in) high. Alternatively, sow them in seed mixture in a seed box, and plant the seedlings out when they are large enough to handle.

If you have a greenhouse or frame you can sow many of the annuals a month early so as to be ready for planting outside when there is no longer any danger of frost.

In dry periods the seedlings need almost constant attention, and careful watering with a fine rose on the watering can. Hand weeding between the tiny plants is important, too.

Many of the annual herbs only take from two to three months to flower, and if planted out at the beginning of the summer, will be ready to harvest at the end of it. *Borago officinalis* (borage) and *Satureia hortensis* (savory) ripen particularly quickly (and borage will seed itself happily all over the garden).

If you feel growing from seed entails too much time and trouble, do not despair, many of these annual herbs, like the perennials, can be bought as plants. Indeed, in temperate climes you may have no alternative to buying small plants for such herbs as French tarragon.

Growing plants and cuttings The perennial herbs, and the annuals, too, if you prefer, are bought as plants or cuttings and put directly into the bed during the summer. Dig a hole with a trowel and if it is dry, fill the whole with water. Put in the plant and firm the soil back down around it so that it is well anchored in case of rain or gale. For the first two weeks protect the young plants from sun and wind and water them carefully every evening.

Care Weeding is even more important in a herb garden than in a flower garden. Each plant, clump, or row must stand alone. They need to be kept neat with no weeds or grass growing near. Label any perennial plants which are going to die down in the winter—or you may forget where they are. Water according to the plants' needs but remember that in very hot weather succulent herbs like mint and chives will need watering three times a day, although normally they would only require watering twice a week; and herbs like sage will need watering every other day in dry weather. In cooler climates, delicate perennials will need mulching to protect them from severe frost.

Growing herbs in containers Position the container in the sun or shade according to the preference of the herb you intend to grow in it. Make sure there are plenty of drainage holes and place a layer of broken clay flower pots or shards in the bottom. Fill to within 2.5cm (1in) with a mixture of five parts garden soil, two parts compost and one and a half parts each of peat and sand. Topdress once a month with organic fertiliser and make sure the plants have plenty of root room. Water according to the plants' needs—overwatering can kill them.

Growing herbs indoors

For those people without a garden, it is perfectly possible to grow most herbs in pots or window boxes. Growing herbs indoors has the added advantage of enabling some herbs to grow all year round which, in cooler climates, would only flourish outdoors in the summer. Although the individual requirements of each herb regarding position, soil type, watering and feeding are given later in the book, here is some general advice.

Which herbs to grow Low-growing herbs are most suitable for pots and window boxes. These could include the following: thyme, tarragon, basil, rosemary, geraniums, chives, mint, parsley, marjoram, oregano and pennyroyal. Larger herbs, such as sage, fennel and borage will tend to become dwarfed naturally if grown in a restricted area. Herbs with a wandering root, such as mint, lemon balm and tarragon need to be grown in individual pots, which can then be placed in a window box.

Position Herbs should be placed in a south- or west-facing window that gets plenty of sun and light. If you turn them around 45° every day they shouldn't become too tall and weedy, or deformed in shape through growing constantly towards the light.

The temperature of the room should not fall below 10°C (50°F) or exceed 16°C (60°F) at night. Herbs do not like sudden changes of temperature, and therefore they should not really be grown in a kitchen.

If your rooms receive little light, this can be achieved with the aid of overhead mercury fluorescent lamps, but natural light is preferable.

Herbs also need plenty of air. Ventilation is particularly necessary if you have gas central heating, but remember that they do not like draughts. If you have a roof, balcony or patio, try to put them outside whenever it is warm. Before balancing pots on window sills, however, check that it is not too windy. A potted plant falling from a great height can be a lethal missile.

Soil The soil for herbs in pots or window boxes is very important. Get a special bag of potting mixture from a nursery or gardening shop, stating what you want it for. A good potting mixture for herbs is one made up of equal parts of sand, leaf mould and soil, although a bay tree is happier in a pot of rich soil. Fill pots or boxes up to 1cm (½in) of the top to leave room for water.

Planting You can now buy ready-to-germinate herbs in small peat pots which make herb gardening even simpler. If these are unobtainable then they may be grown from seed or cuttings according to the instructions in the section on growing herbs outside. Buying small plants, although slightly more expensive, does, of course, produce quicker results. Ordinary clay pots are perfectly suitable so long as you remember to put some broken pots or shards in the bottom to provide good drainage.

Care Apart from ensuring that the temperature is reasonably even and that they are well ventilated the other important points are watering and feeding. Each plant has its individual requirements but watering should also take into account the season and the indoor temperature. Never leave your plants permanently wet and soggy, and allow the soil almost to dry out between waterings. Feed regularly with liquid organic fertiliser, following the manufacturer's instructions carefully. As soon as the roots begin to protrude through the drainage holes, transfer the herb to a larger pot.

Harvesting Never remove more than a fifth of the leaves from one plant at a time and make sure that new leaf growth has begun to form before cutting again.

This rule does not, however, apply to chives, of which all the leaves may be cut at once, so it is a good idea to grow more than one pot.

Finally, although some care and attention is obviously required to grow herbs indoors, the results are extremely rewarding. Healthy herbs look superb and provide you with attractive, aromatic houseplants—as well as being extremely useful.

Herbs grown indoors should be placed in a window which receives as much natural light as possible. Try to remember to turn the plants around completely every day as all plants grow towards the light. If you have access to a patio or balcony, your herbs will benefit from being set outside on warm, sunny days. When harvesting herbs in pots, never remove more than one fifth of the total number of leaves, and wait for new leaf growth to appear before you cut them again.

47

WILD HERBS

'Anything green that grows out of the mould
Was an excellent herb to our fathers of old.'

Rudyard Kipling

Almost any piece of uncultivated land, whether it is a wood or a building site, will yield wild plants which contain both nutritional and healing properties. Alas, when they appear on cultivated land, such as in the garden, we tend to destroy them on the pretext that they are weeds. These properties, and the knowledge of how to use them, were well known to our ancestors, but it is only in recent years that, as research laboratories confirm scientifically what was once learnt through experience and inherited knowledge, we have also been able to make use of the same information. Indeed, many previously 'wild' herbs are now being cultivated for the drug market and are also available in herbalist stores.

However tempting the idea may be of gathering your own herbs from the veritable medicine chest in hedgerows, meadows and fields do be careful. It is important to distinguish between those plants which are good for us and those which are not (if not actively poisonous), and to avoid selecting those plants which have been made harmful by pollution from cars and factories, and from the poisonous chemicals that may have been sprayed on them. Always arm yourself with a good illustrated reference book, and do not risk picking herbs where crop spraying has been going on. If in any doubt about a plant, leave it. A good herbalist will stock many dried wild herbs and should also be able to supply you with the relevant information on how to use them.

However, as collecting wild fruits and berries is becoming an increasingly popular activity, here is a list of the easiest to come by and recognise.

Achilla millefolium
YARROW

Yarrow is one of the most useful of wild herbs as it is an all round remedy, strengthener and antiseptic. It has feathery leaves on tough, ribbed stems and dense, flat clusters of small white, or occasionally pink, flowers. It will grow almost anywhere and assists other plants nearby as it helps them to resist disease. Yarrow grows to a height of 45-60cm (18-24in). The leaves may be used fresh or dried to make tea which helps rheumatism and the circulation. Fresh, young yarrow leaves may be chopped and added to salads and sandwiches. Warmed, and made into a poultice, the leaves were also used to staunch wounds.

Agrimonia eupatoria
AGRIMONY

A common, perennial weed, found in Europe, Asia and Africa, agrimony was used in the past to treat and heal wounds. It grows 60cm (2ft) tall with hairy, pinnate leaves and small yellow flowers in spikes. The infused leaves are a tonic and said to be good for coughs and to purify the blood.

From the time of the ancient Greeks, agrimony (also known as church steeples) has been valued for its medicinal properties, and Culpeper admired its sweet and fruity scent.

Alchemilla vulgaris
LADY'S MANTLE

This pretty, little, low perennial grows in clumps and is found in Europe, Asia and North America. It was a wound herb. The leaves are kidney-shaped and downy, and the small flowers are yellowish green.

The leaves are used and cut when the plant is flowering to be dried and used as a tisane. It is recommended to be taken during the mentrual cycle and pregnancy, and it is also a general tonic. As a skin tonic it is effective against freckles and acne, and the mixture is 1-2 teaspoons of the dried or fresh leaves to a cup of water steeped for ten minutes.

It is easily grown from seed and when established will spread itself readily.

Artemisia vulgaris
MUGWORT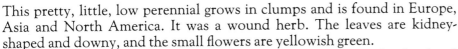

An aromatic plant with dark green, finely cut, downy leaves, dark red stems and small greyish flowers. Mugwort grows to a height of 90-120cm (3-4ft) and is found in fields and hedgerows. The leaves are used, fresh or dried, both cooked with fatty foods like goose and eel and to make a tea which is taken for rheumatism and female complaints. A strong infusion dabbed on the skin is said to repel insects.

Betonica officinalis
BETONY

Betony is a perennial plant found growing wild in woods and hedgerows.

Top and centre Lady's mantle was once known as the 'alchemist's herb' and considered to have almost magical healing properties. Reaching a height of 15-45cm (6-18in) it has yellow-green flowers and is found growing in soil which is moist but well-drained. Above Mugwort grows to a height of about 90cm (3ft). The flower shoots are cut from mid to late summer and the buds used as a seasoning.

It has hairy, toothed leaves and crimson flowers. The tea made from it is aromatic and astringent.

Centaurea cyanus
CORNFLOWER

These familiar, blue-flowered plants may be seen growing wild in corn fields, or cultivated in gardens as pretty summer annuals. The flowers have no scent but are used dried to give colour to *pot-pourri* and also to make an infusion with which to bathe the eyes.

Euphrasia officinalis
EYEBRIGHT

Found growing on dry heaths, pastures, and other poor-soiled open areas of land, eyebright is a small, annual plant about 15cm (6in) high. The tiny flowers are white or lilac, and it needs to grow amongst grass or other plants as it depends on their roots for nourishment. Its use is medicinal. The whole plant is pressed and the juice extracted and used to make an eye lotion.

Hypericum perforatum
ST. JOHN'S WORT

Also known as ragwort, this herbaceous perennial has bright golden, fringed flowers and toothed leaves and grows to 90cm (3ft) high. In the past St. John's wort was thought to keep away evil. St. John himself was also patron saint of horses, and an infusion of leaves was used as a remedy for equine diseases. Nowadays the oil is used to help heal rheumatism, strains, insect bites and bruises, while a tea made from the leaves is said to alleviate fever, depression and insomnia.

Meliotus officinalis
MELILOT

A tall annual with leaves in groups of three and spikes of small, yellow flowers, melilot is found growing in hedgerows and fields all over Europe and Asia. The leaves have a scent reminiscent of newly mown hay, which becomes more intense when dried. Consequently, the dried leaves are sometimes added to *pot-pourri* as well as for making tisanes. The leaves may also be used to give flavour to marinades and dishes made with rabbit or cheese.

Menyanthes trifoliata
BUCK BEAN

Also called bog bean and water or marsh trefoil, this is an aquatic plant found growing on the muddy fringes of pools and ponds and in marshy places. It has clusters of pink, lily-shaped flowers and grows wild in North

America, and in the cooler parts of Asia and Europe. The leaves may be made into a tisane or the roots cooked as a vegetable. It is mainly of medicinal value and used to be recommended as a cure for scurvy.

Plantago major
PLANTAIN

A common, perennial weed in lawns, plantain produces flat rosettes of leaves and spikes of pinky-purple flowers. Both the seeds and leaves are eaten for their medicinal value. The leaves may be applied direct to wounds and stings, and also made into a tea which acts as a diuretic.

Sambucus nigra
ELDER

The elder bush or tree varies in height between 3-10m (9-30ft) and is found growing along hedges and in fields. It is an elegant plant, with cork-like bark, delicate leaves and flat clusters of sweet-smelling, lacy, cream flowers from which develop the rich, dark red berries in the autumn. All parts of the elder are rich in vitamins and capable of utilization. The flowers are used for wine and tea, for cosmetics and lotions; the berries for wine, sauces, jellies and puddings, where they can be used as a substitute for currants, and to cure neuralgia; the roots can be made into an infusion and used as a laxative; and a juice can be extracted from the bark and leaves to use as a dye.

Sedum acre
STONECROP

Stonecrop is a succulent which is found growing wild in rocky and stony places throughout the world but may also be cultivated as a house-plant. It is a low-growing perennial with tiny, yellow flowers. The fresh leaves are too bitter to use, but dried they make an excellent substitute for pepper.

Smyrnium oluestratum
ALEXANDER

A biennial of medium height with yellow-green umbels and small, black, ripe seeds, stonecrop can be found growing on wasteland, particularly near the sea, in most countries. The young shoots and leaf stems have a celery-like taste and may be cooked as a vegetable. At one time it was widely cultivated as a pot herb and is a useful addition to soups and stews.

Spiraea ulmaria
MEADOW SWEET

A common, perennial plant with serrated leaves, clusters of small, creamy, sweet-smelling flowers and red stems, meadow sweet can be found growing wild in marshy fields and along river banks in Asia, Europe and America. In the Middle Ages it was a popular strewing herb, but nowadays the

Top There are about 260 varieties of plantain, mainly small plants under 15cm (6in) high with tiny, insignificant flowers. Once prized as a herb with healing properties, plantain is now, alas, almost universally regarded as a weed. Above Elder berries are picked in early autumn and used for wine-making and in jams and tarts with apple.

leaves are generally made into a tisane which acts as a diuretic and is reputedly good for colds.

Stellaria media
CHICKWEED

A ubiquitous annual found growing all over the temperate world, chickweed is generally regarded as a weed. It is a low, sprawling plant with white flowers which seeds itself and flowers again so quickly that it is about virtually throughout the year. Full of nutrients, the whole plant may be chopped and added to salads and sandwiches. It has a salty, fresh flavour and may also be cooked and served as a vegetable. Chickweed acts as a diuretic and made into an ointment is said to cure chilblains.

Taraxacum officinale
DANDELION

A distinctive plant about 25cm (10in) high with green serrated leaves and spiky yellow flowers, the dandelion is easily recognized. It is very nutritious and contains vitamins, proteins and minerals, so it is fortunate that dandelion is a perennial and found growing almost everywhere. The leaves may be used raw in salads or cooked as a vegetable, and to make dandelion and burdock wine. The roots are toasted and used as a substitute for coffee. The creamy white liquid exuded by the whole plant can be made into a tisane, which like the teas made from the leaves, is good for digestive upsets and for rheumatism.

Tussilago farfara
COLTSFOOT

One of the prettiest of weeds, coltsfoot is a hardy perennial found growing on wasteland in towns, banks and ditches—in fact, anywhere. It has fringed, yellow, daisy flowers on scaly stalks which appear in spring and fragrant leaves which do not appear until after the flowers have died. Coltsfoot is rich in vitamin C (but was used as a medicinal herb long before people understood nutritional values). Both the leaves and the flowers may be dried and used in wine or to make tisanes. The Latin name for coltsfoot means 'cough' and an infusion of the leaves of this plant is one of the oldest remedies for catarrh, coughs and other similar chest complaints.

Urtica dioica
NETTLE

One of the commonest and easily recognized of weeds throughout the temperate regions of the world, the nettle has many medicinal and nutritional properties. The plants are about 1-1.5m (3-5ft) high, perennial and have dark green leaves covered with stinging hairs. They thrive almost anywhere but particularly where the soil is rich in nitrogen. The young leaves have a salty flavour and may be added to salads after blanching, or boiled as a vegetable. Fresh or dried the leaves make an excellent tisane which acts as a blood purifier and, because they contain vitamin C, as a preventative against colds.

Top and above *Dandelions are very nutritious and, with their distinctive flowers, are easily recognizable. The flowers may be used for making wine, and the leaves used fresh in salads or fresh or dried for tisanes, while the ground, roasted roots are used as a substitute for coffee.*

A CONCISE
HERBAL

Allium sativum
GARLIC

Garlic is not a herb in the botanical sense of the word, being a member of the onion group and therefore a vegetable. However, because of its use in cooking and medicine it is treated as such. The plant has long, flat leaves and a bunch of small, white, star-shaped flowers at the top of each flower stem. The bulb is a collection of 'cloves' held together by the outer skin. A garlic plant reaches a height of about 30cm (12in).

Soil Well-drained, rich.

Position Full sun.

Planting and cultivation Split a garlic bulb into cloves and plant each clove, pointed end up, 5cm (2in) deep and 20cm (8in) apart. Leave 30cm (12in) between each row. Weed well by hand.

Harvesting In later summer, when the stems and leaves have lost their greenness and have toppled over, lift the garlic bulbs with a fork and spread them out in a warm, dry, sunny place to dry and ripen off. Don't try to pull them out, as any damage done to the stems tends to cause the bulbs to rot. After several days, store the garlic bulbs in string bags and use as required.

Propagation From cloves saved from previous year's crop.

Pot growth Not suitable.

Uses Medicinally garlic is reputed to aid the digestion, reduce high blood pressure, expel catarrh from the chest and act as an antiseptic. Except when boiled, garlic is strong so use with discretion in cooking. It is used crushed in salad dressings and crushed or whole in meat, fish, poultry dishes, soups, stews and vegetable dishes. The mainstay of much Italian cooking and also French, it is particularly used in combination with parsley, with which it has a great affinity.

The attractive pinky-purple flowers of the chive plant are normally cut off in order to promote the growth of new leaves.

Allium schoenoprasum
CHIVES

Like garlic, the chive is a member of the onion group but again is treated as a herb. This hardy perennial is native to the temperate climes of Europe and North America. It has thin, hollow, grass-like leaves, reaching about 25cm (10in) in height, and pretty, pinky-purple flowers. The leaves have the most delicate flavour of any member of the onion family. The clumps grow from clusters of tiny, flat bulbs.

Soil Rich, moist alkaline soils.

Position Semi-shade.

Planting and cultivation Easily grown from seeds sown in spring or early summer in drills 1cm ($\frac{1}{2}$in) deep and 30cm (12in) apart. Thin seedlings to 15cm (6in) apart. Do not allow the plant to flower if you want a continual source of fresh leaves. Water well and give a little organic fertilizer from time to time.

Harvesting Cut the leaves with scissors as and when they are needed to about 3cm (1in) above soil level. Cut clumps in succession to ensure a constant supply. Chives do not dry well but freeze successfully.

Propagation Multiplies rapidly underground. Every three to four years divide during the autumn into clumps of about six bulblets and replant.

Pot growth Grows well in pots, needing one with an ultimate diameter of 18cm (7in).

Uses In cooking, wherever a mild oniony taste is required; in salads, cheese or egg dishes, over soups and cooked vegetables, especially new and jacket potatoes and even on bread and butter. Use generously with any except the most delicate of vegetables.

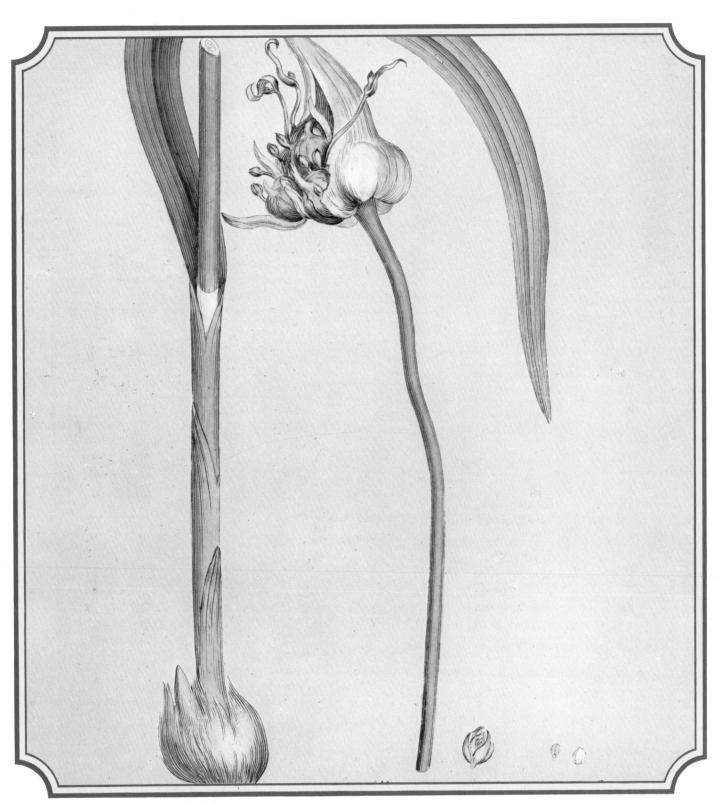

Above *Garlic is treated as a herb, although, like the chive, it is strictly a vegetable.* Far left *Garlic produces bunches of small white flowers at the top of each flower stem.* Left *To harvest garlic, the whole plant should be carefully lifted with a fork and spread out in a warm, sunny place to dry and ripen off.*

Plate 496.

The angelica plant is one of the tallest of herbs, reaching a height of about 2m (6ft). It has large serrated leaves with an attractive scent and strong, ridged stems. Towards the end of summer, it produces beautiful umbels of flowers which are particularly unusual in that they are yellow-green in colour.

Angelica archangelica

ANGELICA

One of the tallest and most decorative of herbs, angelica is a biennial that becomes almost a perennial if the seeds are allowed to sow themselves. It grows to about 2m (6ft) high and has large indented leaves with a strong fragrance and strong, ridged stems. Beautiful umbels of green flowers appear in late summer.

Soil A rich, moist soil.

Position Semi-shady and open. Angelica withstands moderate frosts.

The leaves of the angelica plant can be made into a tisane and either drunk or applied to the face as a skin tonic. The stems are candied and used for decoration and flavouring and should be cut before the plant flowers.

Planting and cultivation Seeds sown in late summer will produce stalks for candying by the following summer when fresh seeds may be sown. Plants which are allowed to flower and seed themselves will soon produce seedlings to plant out the following spring. Angelica plants should be watered regularly and the soil dressed with compost. If the stems need to develop further before they are ready for harvesting, then the flowers should be removed, as once the plant has flowered it dies.

Harvesting Cut leaves as required during the early summer. The stems should be harvested before the plant flowers.

Propagation By root division and sowing seeds.

Uses The leaves, fresh or dried, may be infused in boiling water for a tisane or as a basis for a skin tonic. The dried leaves also make an attractive and fragrant addition to *pot-pourris*. The stems may be candied and then used both for cake decoration and to flavour food, such as jam. Infusions of angelica were also reputed to be a protection against the plague and dog bites.

Anthriscus cerefolium CHERVIL

Although an annual, by successional sowing, fresh chervil may be harvested for most of the year. Similar in appearance to parsley but more delicate, it

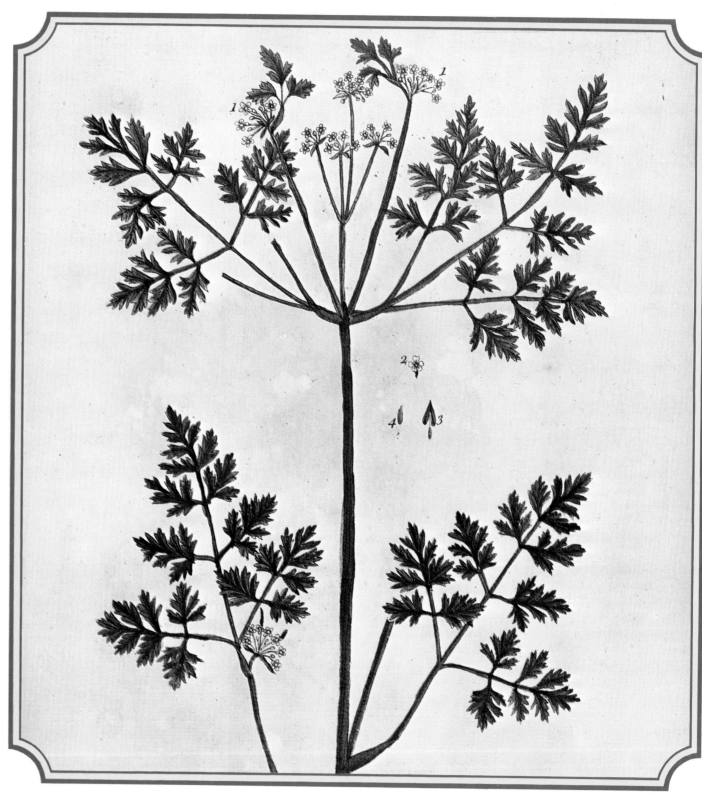

Chervil is similar in appearance to parsley but is more delicate and fern-like. The fresh, green leaves, with their slight flavour of aniseed, may be substituted for parsley or chives and sprinkled over salads and soups. It is one of the principal ingredients of fines herbes and is used with egg, cheese and fish dishes and in liqueurs.

has pale green, fern-like leaves and small white flowers, and reaches a height of about 60cm (2ft). The leaves have a slightly sweet flavour of aniseed and it is a particulatrly popular herb in France. It dislikes hot, dry climates.

Soil Most soils that are light and moist but well drained.

Position Chervil prefers semi-shade in the heat of the summer and full sun in the spring and autumn.

Planting and cultivation Sow a little seed from early spring onwards at regular intervals. The plants take about four weeks to mature. Press the seed gently into the ground in drills about 30cm (12in) apart. Thin the seedlings to 20cm (5in) apart. Always keep slightly moist. To prevent chervil running to seed too quickly, try to pick off any flowers as they appear.

Harvesting The leaves are ready to pick about six weeks after sowing; pick before the flowers bloom. Not suitable for drying.

Propagation By seed.

Pot growth Grows well in pots or window boxes, provided it is kept moist.

Uses Use the leaves generously in cooking wherever you would use parsley. Chervil is best added to food at the last moment. It is an important constituent of *fines herbes* and sometimes of *bouquet garni*. It is particularly good in salads, soups, dressings and in fish and egg dishes.

Finely chopped and warmed, and then applied as a poultice to bruises and sprained joints, chervil leaves are said to relieve pain.

Artemisia abrotanum
SOUTHERNWOOD

Also known as lad's love, this small perennial shrub can reach a height of 90cm (3ft). It is a native of southern France where it can be found growing wild. It has a woody stem and feathery, grey-green leaves covered with down. The flowers, which rarely appear in temperate climes, are yellow. The leaves of southernwood have a highly attractive aroma and a bitter lemon taste. Southernwood was traditionally grown in herb gardens to keep witches out but nowadays is grown mostly for its appearance.

Soil Sandy, light and well drained.

Position Sunny.

Planting and cultivation Plant in late autumn or early spring and leave 38cm (15in) between each plant. Each spring the plant should be pruned to within two buds from the ground.

Harvesting Cut branches at the end of summer and dry them.

Propagation Take 25cm (10in) cuttings in spring.

Pot growth Will grow well in tubs and is suitable for towns as it is not adversely affected by fumes.

Uses Southernwood is rarely used in cooking although the shoots are occasionally added to cakes. The dried stems are, however, put in bags and used in clothes' cupboards to repel moths or as an ingredient of *pot-pourri*. Infused in boiling water, southernwood makes a refreshing tisane which acts as a tonic and is reputed to cure worms. The leaves of this plant should never be eaten as they are very poisonous.

Artemisia dracunculus
TARRAGON

Both varieties of tarragon, French (*A. dracunculus*) and Russian (*A. dracunculoides*) are shrubby perennials which become larger each year. French tarragon is slightly more difficult to grow but has a far superior taste to that of Russian and so is the only one worth growing. French tarragon comes from the Middle East and grows to a height of about 1m (3ft). The French variety has widely spaced leaves on the stems from which the clusters of whitish flowers also grow. The leaves are smoother, darker and shinier than those of Russian tarragon.

Soil Light and well drained.

Position Full sun.

Planting and cultivation French tarragon can almost never be grown from seed but only from root divisions or cuttings. Plant these in the spring, when there is no danger of frost, about 45-60cm (18-24in) apart. The root system becomes quite large so the plants need a lot of room. Protect plants

Southernwood is a perennial shrub with beautiful, silvery-grey foliage. The dried leaves and stems not only smell lovely but also repel insects such as moths. Consequently, these are often put in sachets and used to protect and scent clothes and linen.

from frost in winter. French tarragon deteriorates after about four years so plants should be divided and replanted, or replaced by new plants, after this time.

Harvesting Use fresh leaves as required in the summer and autumn. Cut stems for drying in mid-summer.

Propagation By root division or cuttings.

Pot growth Can be grown successfully indoors in pots with an ultimate diameter of 30cm (12in). Care must be taken, however, to ensure good drainage. Tarragon will not tolerate wet roots.

Uses The leaves are one of the main ingredients in Béarnaise, Hollandaise and Tartare sauces. They are also excellent cooked or raw with chicken, fish, some salads, tomato soup and some meats and vegetables. Tarragon leaves are, of course, used in tarragon vinegar, and also in several stuffings, in *fines herbes*, marinades and with egg dishes. Excessive use of dried tarragon can produce a slightly bitter flavour.

Asperula odorata
WOODRUFF

A low, carpeting perennial with ruff-like leaves in whorls and white, star-shaped flowers. It grows 15-30cm (6-12in) high in shady woodland. Woodruff has shiny leaves and a scent like that of freshly mown hay.

Soil Damp and full of humus—like that found in a wood.

Position Shady, under trees and bushes.

Planting and cultivation As the seeds can take as long as a year to germinate, it is more satisfactory to plant rootstock or young plants in spring with 20cm (8in) spaces between them. Once established it will form a carpet and as it is self-seeding will not need replacing.

Harvesting The plants develop their full scent when first picked and beginning to dry. Sprigs should be picked in spring before or during flowering and dried at a low temperature so that they stay green. Use fresh leaves as required.

Propagation By seed and root division.

Pot growth Quite suitable if the plant is kept moist and shaded.

Uses Woodruff leaves are added to summer drinks, such as fruit cups, white wine and apple juice. It is also made into tisanes and is supposed to lift the spirits. Like southernwood, woodruff can be strewn amongst linen both for its attractive fragrance and for its power to repel insects.

The fresh leaves of the borage plant, with their faint cucumber-like flavour, are added to cold, summer drinks, especially Pimms, and to salads.

Borago officinalis
BORAGE

The name is derived from the latin *burra*, meaning rough hair. This refers to the rough hairs on the stems and large, grey-green leaves of the plant. Borage, a sturdy annual, originates from the Mediterranean, and grows to a height of about 60-90cm (2-3ft) tall. It has vivid blue flowers which grow in drooping clusters and is very attractive to bees. Both the flowers and the leaves are edible, the leaves having a faint cucumber-like flavour.

Soil Most soils, but preferably chalky or sandy.

Position Sunny.

Planting and cultivation The seeds should be grown at 45cm (18in) intervals in spring and covered well with soil. They germinate quickly and reach maturity within five to six weeks. Once the plants are established they sow themselves so there is no need to replace plants. Borage plants continue to bloom throughout the year in mild climates and until the first

frost elsewhere.

Harvesting Use fresh leaves and flowers as required. It does not respond well to drying.

Propagation By seed and root division.

Pot growth Not recommended for pots but will grow in large window boxes.

Uses The flowers may be candied and used for cake decoration. The leaves are used in drinks, especially wine cups, such as Pimms, with apple juice, in salads and cooked with cabbage. Borage makes a refreshing tisane, iced or hot, which is reputed to have a wonderful effect on both the mind and body and dispels depression.

With its vivid blue, star-shaped flowers, which grow in drooping clusters, and its large, furry, grey-green leaves, borage is a particularly enchanting herb. The flowers, which are very attractive to bees, are added to pot-pourri to give colour and have always been a popular motif in embroidery. They may be candied like violets.

Marigolds have been cultivated in herb gardens from ancient times and are one of the easiest and most rewarding of flowers to grow. Their glorious bright orange flowers are a colourful addition to any garden and if the dead flowers are picked off regularly the plants will bloom throughout the summer and into the autumn.

Calendula officinalis
MARIGOLD

An annual with familiar, bright, daisy flowers with petals ranging in colour from pale yellow to a deep, rich orange. Marigold can reach a height of about 50cm (20in) depending on the variety. The plant is thought to have originated in India and may be seen today growing wild in the fields and vineyards of southern Europe.

Commercially available marigold plants tend to be double-flowered and are easy to grow in beds or window boxes and pots.

Soil Any kind of soil but preferably loam.

Position Full sun.

Planting and cultivation Sow seeds in spring and thin seedlings to 45cm (18in) apart. Marigold plants will re-seed themselves but tend to revert to single heads if allowed to do so.

Harvesting Only the petals are used and these may be fresh or dried. To dry, place in thin layers at a low temperature in a dark, airy place so that they retain their colour.

Propagation By seed.

Pot growth Seeds or young plants will grow well in pots and windows boxes.

Uses In cooking, marigold petals can be substituted for saffron, for instance in saffron rice. They produce the same colour effect but not the same flavour. They are a colourful addition to salads and are also used in omelettes and stews. Soaked in oil, they are reputed to aid the complexion if rubbed on the skin, and heal wounds. Made into a tisane, they are said to remedy digestive problems and improve the complexion.

Carum carvi
CARAWAY

Although the caraway plant is a herb, its seeds are generally treated as a spice. It is a biennial with delicate, ferny leaves and white umbels of flowers. The ripe fruits of these flowers split into two seeds. The caraway plant grows to a height of about 60cm (2ft) and is widely grown in Russia, Europe, Scandinavia, India and North America.

Soil Most soils if they are dry and well-drained.

Position Sunny.

Planting and cultivation Sow seeds in spring and thin to 23cm (9in) apart. Prune plants in the autumn. They need little care other than weeding and ensuring that they have water in very dry weather. Plants will flower and go to seed in the summer of the following year. The roots are delicate and so the seed should be sown *in situ* to avoid transplanting. Once established caraway will seed itself.

Harvesting When the seeds are ripe, cut off the plants at ground level and hang up in sheaves in a dry, airy place. When the seeds have dried they can be shaken off on to paper and stored in airtight jars.

Propagation By seed.

Pot growth Not recommended.

Uses The seeds are delicious cooked in seed cakes, with fatty meats such as goose and pork, and particularly with cabbage dishes, carrots and cheese. It is an important ingredient of Kümmel and other liqueurs. The roots may be boiled and eaten as a vegetable, while the tender young leaves add a refreshing taste to salads and soup. Made into a tisane, caraway is said to aid the digestion.

Chrysanthemum balsamita or *Tanacetum balsamita*
COSTMARY or ALECOST

A medium-sized perennial, dying down each winter and coming up again each spring. The leaves are long and thin and have a scent of mint and a flavour of lemon. The leaves are grey-green in colour while the flowers are white with yellow centres and grow in clusters. The name alecost dates from the time when it was used in the preparation of home-brewed ale.

Soil Any well-drained soil.

Position Sunny.

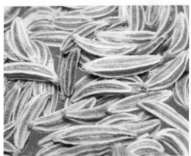

Top The petals of marigolds are used in cooking both for their colour and their flavour. They may be used in salads and omelettes and as a cheaper alternative to saffron. Centre The caraway plant with its ferny leaves and white flowers should be grown in situ as it reacts badly to transplanting. Both the leaves and seeds are used in cooking. Above Caraway seeds are treated as a spice and used to flavour both food and liqueurs.

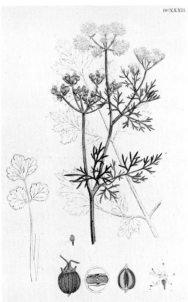

Planting and cultivation Buy a small plant and plant in spring. Costmary originates from the East and will not grow from seed in temperate climes. Take care that its extensive root system does not damage those of more delicate plants, and chop the roots back regularly.

Harvesting Pick leaves as required and dry or use fresh.

Propagation By root division.

Pot growth Not recommended.

Uses The fresh leaves may be used in brewing beer, in stuffings and to make tisanes. The dried leaves are occasionally added to *pot-pourri*.

Cochlearia armoracia

HORSERADISH

Horseradish is a hardy perennial member of the mustard family. Originating from eastern Europe, it was for many years regarded as a medicine rather than as a condiment. The leaves and stems contain a poisonous substance but the white, fleshy root is safe to eat and high in vitamin C. Horseradish is extremely easy to grow and reaches a height of about 60cm (2ft).

Soil Rich, deep, moist soil, preferably with plenty of manure worked in.

Position Sunny or semi-shade.

Planting and cultivation Plant horseradish crowns in the spring leaving 30cm (12in) between them. Keep the bed weed free to allow the roots to develop and pick off flower buds as they appear. Horseradish spreads rapidly so it is advisable to dig up the whole bed when harvesting and replant the following spring.

Harvesting Lift all roots in the autumn when they are about 25cm (10in) long. Store smaller, thinner thongs in sand to plant next spring.

Propagation By root division as the seed pods rarely mature.

Pot growth Not suitable.

Uses It is used principally raw and grated to make the condiment horseradish sauce which is excellent with beef. It does, however, have strong antibiotic properties and is reputed to prevent scurvy.

Top *Horseradish will grow easily in most rich soils. The leaves cannot be eaten but the roots, as well as having antibiotic qualities, have a delicious flavour and can be made into a sauce which tastes particularly good with beef.* Above *The pungent, aromatic seeds of coriander can be included in soups, ground over meat and used to flavour vinegars and vegetable dishes.*

Coriandrum sativum

CORIANDER

This hardy annual herb is grown both for its small round seeds, which are used as a spice, and for its glossy, dark green, feathery leaves. Coriander grows to a height of about 60cm (2ft) and bears pale pinky-mauve flowers. The leaves and unripe seeds have an unpleasant smell which fortunately disappears as ripeness sets in.

Soil Fertile and well drained; and preferably manured the year prior to planting. Do not plant in recently manured soil.

Position Sunny.

Planting and cultivation Sow seeds in early spring for mature plants by the summer. Self-sown seedlings often appear in later summer. Thin seedlings to 10cm (4in) apart.

Harvesting Do not harvest until you are sure the seeds are fully ripe, that is when the fruits have turned from green to grey. Cut the plants and leave for a day or two on the ground to complete ripening. Shake out the seeds of the plants and store.

Propagation By seed.

Uses The seeds are used whole and grown to flavour confectionery, liqueurs, curry powders, sauces, pickles, desserts and breads. The fresh, young leaves are chopped like parsley and used to garnish and flavour,

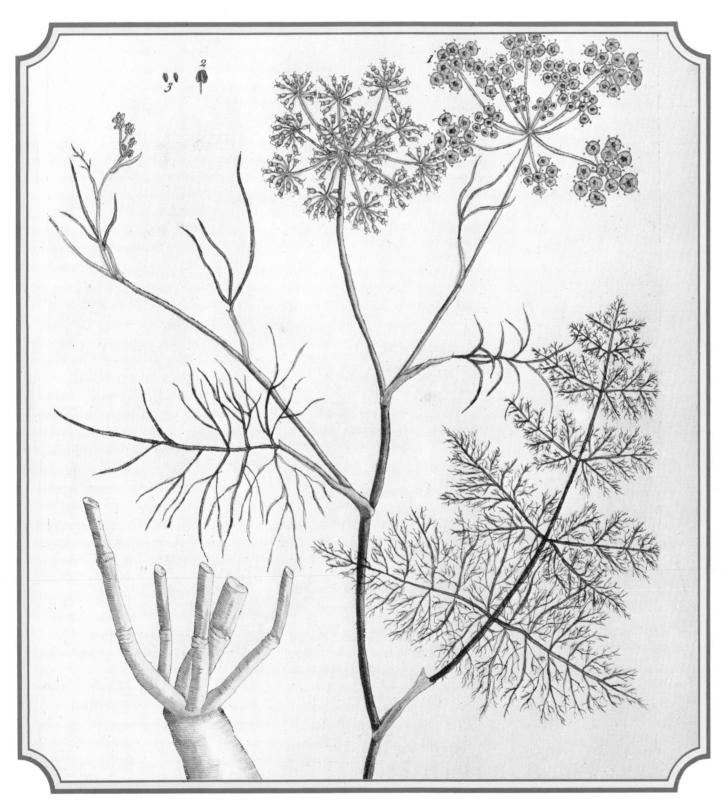

soups, salads, curries, stews and cooked meats and vegetables, especially in India, Greece and Mexico.

Foeniculum vulgare FENNEL

Fennel is native to southern Europe, and although a perennial normally it may need to be treated as an annual in temperature climes. Tall, sometimes, reaching 1.5m (5ft) or more, it has beautiful, yellow-green, feathery leaves

Fennel, with its feathery foliage and yellow umbels of flowers, is a tall, decorative plant. An infusion made from the seeds makes a soothing lotion for the eyes, but it is for its culinary use that it is generally grown. Resembling dill in flavour, fennel leaves are used fresh, but the stems and seeds are dried and used to make gripewater.

and umbels of flowers of the same colour. Although similar to dill in appearance it has a more distinct flavour of aniseed.

Soil Most well drained soils.

Position Sunny.

Planting and cultivation Sow seeds in shallow drills in early spring 5cm (2in) deep and thin seedlings to 40cm (16in) apart. They may need some support against the wind as they become larger. Pinch out all flower buds as they develop. Do not plant near dill as cross pollination may occur. In the autumn cut plants down to 10cm (4in) above the ground. Transplant clumps to pots and bring indoors to prolong harvesting.

Harvesting Pick fresh leaves as required, gather flower heads for seeds in the autumn before they are completely ripe and dry slowly on paper to complete ripening. Shake off the seeds when ripe and store.

Propagation Propagate by lifting pieces of root in spring when they first begin to shoot and replant 30cm (12in) away.

Pot growth Grows well in tubs, window boxes and large pots.

Uses Particularly good with fish, and in marinades, soups, sauces and salads. The seeds are also used in cooking.

Hyssopus officinalis
HYSSOP

Hyssop is a hardy perennial, herbaceous shrub which is partially evergreen. The whole plant is very aromatic and it grows to a height of about 60cm (2ft) making it very attractive as a low hedge. Hyssop has dark green, slim, pointed leaves and deep blue flowers. This highly decorative plant is attractive to bees.

Soil Well-drained ordinary garden soil.

Position Sunny.

Planting and cultivation Sow seeds in spring, or put in plants in the spring or autumn. Transplant seedlings to their final position as soon as they are large enogh to handle. If you are cultivating a hedge, trim it into shape in the autumn.

Harvesting Harvest just as the flowers begin to bloom.

Propagation By cuttings and root division which must be made in the spring or autumn, and by seed.

Pot growth Suitable for growing in a tub or a 25cm (10in) diameter pot.

Uses Hyssop has a strong flavour so use sparingly. Add the tender young growths and flowers to salads. soups and meat, particularly pork. It is an ingredient of Chartreuse and the shoots and leaves make a fragrant tisane which was used as an expectorant and for use in chest complaints.

Juniperus communis
JUNIPER

Juniper is a hardy, perennial shrub which occasionally grows to the size of a small tree and may be found growing wild in Europe, North America and Asia. It has reddish stems and needle-like leaves and the whole plant is highly aromatic.

Soil Any well-drained chalk or limey soil.

Position Juniper favours hill-sides and does not like deep shade.

Planting and cultivation Sow seed or set out small plants in spring, 1.2m (4ft) apart. It is necessary to have two plants as it is very rare to find male and female flowers growing on the same bush. The male flowers resemble green catkins, while the female flowers are cone-like. Although juniper will thrive in extremely barren conditions it responds well to moderate doses

Hyssop, with its bright blue or sometimes pink or even white, flowers, is ideal for borders in the herb garden. It grows to a height of about 60cm (2ft) and is happy in most locations although it prefers a sunny place in light soil. The leaves have a slightly bitter, minty flavour and should be used sparingly in cooking. Regular consumption of a tisane made from the leaves is said to relieve coughs and chest complaints.

of organic fertiliser which will promote growth.

Harvesting The berries should be picked in the autumn when they have turned black. They begin by being green in colour and may take two to three years to mature fully. Use fresh or dry.

Propagation By cuttings or by seed, three of which are contained in each berry. The seeds are slow to germinate.

Pot growth Suitable if grown in a large pot or tub.

Uses To flavour spirits, particularly gin, and food. Good in marinades and with pork, beet, venison and poultry. Medicinally it is reputed to be an effective diurectic and may be taken for this purpose either raw or infused with hot water to make a tisane.

Juniper is a shrub which occasionally grows to the size of a tree. The whole plant is aromatic, from the reddish stems to the needle-like leaves and spicy berries which grow on them. The berries are used to flavour gin, to make tisanes and to flavour marinades for pork, beef, venison and poultry dishes and to make beer.

The bay tree is sacred to Apollo and the leaves have been a symbol of honour for poets, soldiers and athletes alike. A mature tree may grow to 4.75m (12ft) tall or more over twenty years. It has small, yellow flowers in spring, followed by purplish berries, but it is the aromatic leaves which are important for their use in cooking.

Laurus nobilis
SWEET BAY

The sweet bay is an evergreen, shrub-like tree with shiny leathery pointed leaves. A native of Mediterranean lands, it was used particularly by the Romans for making garlands to honour poets, soldiers and atheletes. It has unsignificant flowers which are followed immediately by little black round fruits; but it is the aromatic leaves which are important.

Soil Most soils that are well-drained and dryish.
Position Semi-shade though will withstand full sun.

Planting and cultivation Plant small established plants and try not to move them from their original positions. Young plants should be protected from frost with sacking. Many people train young bushes into various shapes, such as pyramids or balls. This is done by wiring branches into the appropriate position and pinching out unwanted new shoots.

Harvesting Pick fresh leaves as required. When drying leaves, do so in darkness to ensure that they retain their colour.

Pot growth An ideal herb for tubs and large pots. Use a 38-45cm (15-18in) pot with ordinary potting mixture. In temperature climes bring the pot or tub indoors during the winter.

Uses Apart from being reputed to ward off evil its principal use is culinary. A bay leaf is one of the principal ingredients of *bouquet garni*, and it is also used in marinades, pâtés, meat and fish stocks, and soups and stews.

Lavandula spica (syn. *L. officinalis*)
LAVENDER

The word lavender is derived from the latin *lavo*, to wash, since the Romans and the Greeks used lavender to scent their bath water. This perennial shrub has tiny flowers, in shades of blue and purple, clustered on spikes which stand up above the grey-green, narrow-leaved foliage. Lavender bushes are frequently used to make low-growing hedges which smell and look beautiful and attract bees.

Soil Well-drained, limey soil.

Position Open and sunny.

Planting and cultivation Although lavender can be grown from seed it takes a long time. So it is better to buy young plants and plant them in the spring or autumn. Set the plants about 30cm (12in) apart and do not give them too much water. Do not let the flowers go to seed as this encourages them to straggle. After flowering, the bushes should be clipped and shaped, taking care not to cut into the old wood. Trim gently in spring to encourage growth at the base of the plant.

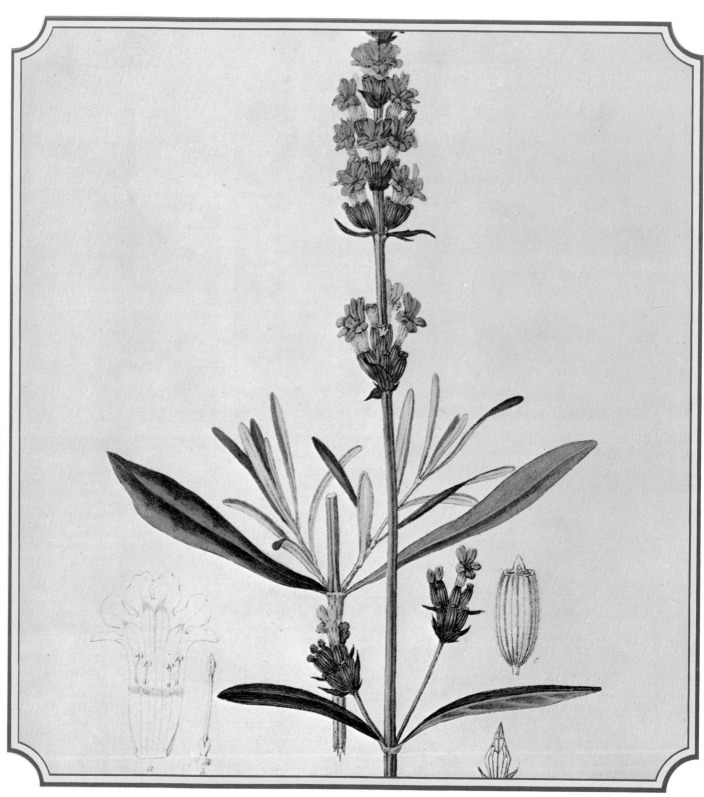

There are many varieties of lavender, but all of them have the same delightful perfumed flowers and leaves. The flowers vary in colour from white, pink, deep blue to pale purple, the most traditional form. The blooms may be used as cut flowers or dried and used in lavender bags or in a pot-pourri both for scent and colour.

Harvesting Gather flower spikes as they come into flower and dry in a warm, 26-38°C (80-100°F), dark place, so that their colour does not fade.

Propagation From cuttings 10-15cm (4-6in) long, taken with a heel in the autumn. Root in a sandy soil mix and plant out the following spring.

Pot growth It is quite possible to grow lavender in large pots and boxes in a suitably sandy, alkaline, soil mix. Protect such plants from frost in winter.

Uses Lavender is not a culinary herb, but its beautiful scent has meant that the essential oil yield from the flowers is used for scent and the dried flower spikes are found in *pot pourri* or made into lavender bags to scent clothes and linen and placed in drawers and closets.

Ligusticum scoticum (syn. *L. officinalis*)
LOVAGE

Lovage is a tall perennial, growing to a height of 2m (6ft), with large, dark, shiny leaves and yellow flowers. It is similar in appearance and scale to angelica.

Soil Deep, rich, wet and preferably organically fertilized.

Position Sunny or semi-shaded.

Planting and cultivation The seed germinates best in darkness and should be sown as soon as it ripens as it quickly loses its germinating power.

Lovage is an extremely vigorous herb, reaching a height of up to 2m (6ft) when in flower. However, unless you want the plant to flower in order to produce seed, it is better to cut off the flower stalks as soon as they have been thrown up from the base as this promotes further leaf production. One plant is sufficient per household.

71

Either sow the seed in spring, in a box or *in situ*, or buy small plants. If you have a greenhouse or frame you can sow a month early so as to be ready for planting outside when there is no danger of frost.

Transplant seedlings, or thin them, to 45cm (18in) apart as soon as they are large enough to handle. Water well. Lovage takes about four years to reach full size and one plant will normally be sufficient per household. Unless you want more seed, cut off to flower stalks to encourage the growth of leaves.

Harvesting Use fresh leaves as required. Drying the thick leaves is difficult but possible and takes about four to five days. Gather seeds as they ripen.

Propagation By seed, or by root division in spring.

Pot growth Not recommended because the roots are so large.

Uses Both the seeds and leaves are used to enrich soups, stews, sauces and salads. The flavour is strong, resembling a cross between celery and yeast, and should be used with discretion. Infused to make a tisane, the leaves are supposed to aid the digestion.

Lippia citriodora

LEMON VERBENA

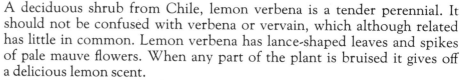

A deciduous shrub from Chile, lemon verbena is a tender perennial. It should not be confused with verbena or vervain, which although related has little in common. Lemon verbena has lance-shaped leaves and spikes of pale mauve flowers. When any part of the plant is bruised it gives off a delicious lemon scent.

Soil Poor, dry soil to which humus has been added.

Position Sunny and sheltered.

Planting and cultivation Although originating from South America, lemon verbena will grow in temperate climes if protected from frost. Buy small plants, put in the ground in spring and water freely except in winter, when the plant is dormant. Pinch out the lead shoots as it grows to stop it straggling. A severe pruning in early spring will help production of leaves. Pot up and move indoors if there is any danger of frost.

Harvesting Collect the leaves as the plant sheds them in the autumn.

Propagation From cuttings of half ripened wood which take easily in spring or summer under glass.

Pot growth A very successful houseplant. Use a standard loam potting mixture.

Uses An essential oil is distilled from its leaves which is used in the preparation of some scents and soaps. A few leaves added to the tea pot will transform ordinary tea, although it also makes a refreshing tisane either alone or with mint. When dried it can be added to *pot pourri*, while fresh it is delightful when cooking if added to lemon sauces, salads, fruit drinks and fruit dishes such as compôtes.

Matricaria chamomilla (Anthemis nobilis)

CHAMOMILE 

There are two plants called chamomile which look very similar. True chamomile, *Matricaria chamomilla* is an annual and the one used for tisanes and cosmetics, while Roman chamomile, *Anthemis nobilis*, is a perennial and used to make sweet-smelling lawns.

Soil Ordinary, dryish soils.

Position Full sun.

Planting and cultivation Sow the seeds of true chamomile in rows at

Although a tisane made from chamomile has a somewhat bitter flavour, it is a very good carminative. A hot infusion of the flowers is also an excellent steam bath for the face, and used as a hair rinse after a shampoo is said to lighten fair hair as well as conditioning it. Chamomile is readily grown from seed.

Right *The tiny white flowers of balm, or lemon balm as it is also known, are particularly attractive to bees, which makes it an ideal plant to grow if you have fruit trees that need cross-pollinating. It is only necessary to grow one balm plant as, like mint, balm has an invasive root system and will spread rapidly once established.*

23cm (9in) intervals. Roman chamomile should be sown as for grass seed to make a lawn. Neither type needs any particular after care.

Harvesting It is only worth picking the pretty blue flowers of true chamomile as they come into bloom. Dry them in an airing cupboard or warm oven and store in a dark place.

Propagation By seed.

Pot growth In window boxes or tubs which allow for lateral spreading.

Uses It is from the flowers of true chamomile that the deep blue oil is extracted which is so good to drink or to use cosmetically. A tisane, made from chamomile will help cure stomach ache and relieve indigestion. An infusion of flowers makes a good conditioning rinse for fair hair, or a steam bath to cleanse the face.

Melissa officinalis
BALM

This hardy, perennial herb, better known as lemon balm, originates from southern Europe and Asia. It derives its name from the Greek word *melissa* meaning a honey bee and does indeed attract these valuable insects by the delightful fragrance of its lemon-scented leaves. Balm has pale green, heart-shaped leaves and small, whitish flowers and forms a shrubby bush about 60-90cm (2-3ft) in height.

Soil Ordinary garden soil.

Position Sunny and sheltered. Leave enough space for the leaves to develop.

Planting and cultivation Either sow seeds or plant cuttings in spring. Balm has an extensive root system so either contain the roots in bottomless buckets submerged in the open ground, or grow in large tubs. Do not allow the plant to flower if you want the leaves for cooking but pinch out the buds as they appear. Weed regularly. In winter cut the plants low and protect from frost where necessary with leaf mould.

Harvesting Pick fresh leaves as required. To dry balm, wait until the end of summer and cut the stems. Tie them in small bunches and hang in an airy place to dry.

Propagation By root division in spring or autumn, or allow it to seed itself.

Uses In cooking, its attractive lemon flavour complements stewed fruit, fish and poultry dishes, stuffings sauces and marinades. It makes a good tisane and is reputed to cure insomnia, soothe the nerves and dispel melancholy. Balm is also used in perfumes, liqueurs and furniture polish, and by bee keepers who rub it on the insides of hives to attract bees.

Mentha
MINT

Mint is a hardy perennial herb remarkable for its aromatic leaves. There are many varieties of mint found widely distributed throughout the world. But the most commonly grown varieties, and the most useful, are as follows; M.*spicata*: spearmint, M.*rotundifolia*: apple or Bowles mint and M.*piperita*: peppermint. All have square stems and white or mauve flowers in spikes and spread rapidly wherever they are planted. Mint originated from the East via North Africa although it is named after the

Mentha piperata (*peppermint*) *is one of the most commonly used herbs. The essential oil is used as an ingredient in toothpaste, confectionery, indigestion tablets and the liqueur crème de menthe. A peppermint tisane is said to aid the digestion. It is one of the few varieties of mint which can be grown from seed and will quickly establish itself.*

Above Bergamot is one of the most decorative of scented herbs. It produces an abundance of aromatic foliage and scarlet flowers. Right Similar in appearance to peppermint but having little or no leaf stalks, spearmint has lilac pink flowers and narrow, thin leaves.

nymph, Minthe, who is reputed to have been turned into this plant. *M.spicata* grows 30-45cm (12-18in) high and has thin, pointed leaves. *M.rotundifolia* has a broader, fleshier and slightly hairy leaf and can grow to 60-120cm (2-4ft) high. *M.piperita* is thinner and is pale green to red in colour. With the exception of *M.rotundifolia*, all mints are prone to rust disease.

Soil Very moist and well dug.

Position Sun or partial shade.

Planting and cultivation Plant roots of all varieties in spring or autumn. Control spreading by restricting roots in a clay pot or old bucket sunk in the ground. Pinch out flower buds on appearance to maintain maximum leaf growth. Renew beds every three to four years by pulling up roots, dividing them and replanting. Keep free from weeds. If rust disease occurs, destroy the bed and start a fresh one.

Harvesting Pick fresh leaves as required and cut for drying when the flowers are in bud. Dry on or off the stems in a dark, well ventilated room at a temperature of about 23°C (73°F).

Propagation By root division in spring or autumn.

Pot growth Will grow in large pots or window boxes in good moist soil. Keep plants pinched down to about 15cm (6in).

Uses Used particularly by the British to make mint sauce or jelly for roast lamb. Also good with boiled vegetables such as potatoes and carrots, and chopped raw into salads and fruit drinks. The dried leaves can be added to *pot-pourri*, and tisanes made from mint, especially peppermint, taste excellent and aid the digestion.

Monarda didyma
BERGAMOT

Originating from North America, this perennial herb is both decorative and fragrant. Bergamot grows to a height of about 60-90cm (2-3ft) and has serrated leaves and spiky flowers whose colours range from white, pink and mauve through to red. Like balm, it is particularly attractive to bees.

Soil Rich and moist.

Position Sun or partial shade.

Planting and cultivation Plant small plants in spring or autumn and top dress the soil, or sow seed out of doors in a semi-shaded position. Seeds germinate easily but discard any drab coloured plants which result. Dig up, divide the roots and replant every two to three years. Water well.

Harvesting The flowers and leaves may be used fresh or dried. Drying should be done in darkness to preserve colour.

Propagation By root division in spring, cuttings in autumn or by seed.

Pot growth Possible with young plants, but will need an enormous tub as they get larger and lots of water.

Uses Both the leaves and flowers can be chopped and added with advantage to salads and pork dishes. The flowers make beautiful table decorations and last for about a week. The commonest use is as tea, either on its own (as drunk by the Oswego Indians) or added to Indian tea.

Myrrhis odorata
SWEET CICELY

A pretty perennial herb, Sweet Cicely takes several years to reach its full height of 150cm (5ft). It is the first herb to appear in spring and the last to die down in the autumn, and so can be used fresh for nearly the whole year. It has large, feathery leaves and umbels of white flowers. The sweet smell and taste of this herb is reminiscent of aniseed.

Soil Any well drained and nourished soil.

Position Partial shade.

Planting and cultivation Either buy and plant small plants or sow seed in spring. Only lightly cover the seed and keep weed free. Leave 45cm (18in) between each plant and pinch out flower buds as they appear to stimulate leaf growth. If allowed to flower this herb will quickly seed itself.

Harvesting Pick fresh leaves as required and leaves for drying in the spring.

Propagation By seed, or by root division in the spring or autumn.

Pot growth Not really suitable, but could be grown outside in a tub as it has large roots.

Uses The roots can be cooked and used as a vegetable. Chopped fresh leaves can be added to salads or stewed with fruit. As it is very sweet, this herb will reduce the amount of sugar normally added to stewed fruit. The leaves may also be added to perfume bath water.

Ocimum basilicum
BASIL

Originating from India, basil is a delicate plant extremely sensitive to frosts and is safer grown indoors in cooler climates where it should be treated as an annual. There are two basic varieties, sweet basil and bush basil. Sweet basil is larger, more aromatic and subtler in flavour than bush basil, and produces white flowers. The scent of sweet basil is said to drive away flies.

Soil Rich and well drained.

Position Sunny and sheltered.

Planting and cultivation Sow sees in early spring, under glass in areas which do not have tropical climates. Grow in sterilized soil as they are prone to 'damping off' disease. Keep seedlings warm and protected. Plant out in early summer in a sheltered border. Remove flowers as they appear to prolong the growth of fresh leaves.

Propagation By seed.

Harvesting Cut leaves for use as needed. It changes flavour when dried.

Pot growth Choose dwarf varieties and keep transplanting to large pots as they grow.

Uses Usually associated in cooking with tomatoes, both raw and cooked, particularly in the form of salads and soups. Equally good with egg dishes, on pizzas and in other Italian dishes.

As dried basil does not retain the same delicate, yet peppery, flavour of the fresh herb, it really is worth growing some in a pot or garden. A few chopped leaves added to some sliced tomatoes and left to marinate for an hour or so before serving is one of the most delicious salads.

Left *Sweet marjoram has reddish stems, small leaves and pinky-white flowers. It may be substituted for oregano in recipes. The leaves are at their best just before the plant flowers. Right Oregano, like all members of this family, is easily grown from seed and responds well to drying.*

Origanum

MARJORAM and OREGANO

There are many different varieties of *Origanum*, each with the same characteristic scent and flavour. The most popular are O. *vulgare*, oregano, O. *onites*, pot marjoram and O. *marjorana*, sweet marjoram. Although all three are perennials O. *marjorana* should be regarded as an annual in cooler climates.

Soil Light, well drained and slightly acidic.

Position Full sun.

Planting and cultivation All varieties can be grown from seed sown in spring in boxes or buy small plants. Do not plant outside in temperate climes until all danger of frost is over. Thin seedlings to 23cm (9in) apart. Water well and protect perennial varieties from frost in winter. Cut regularly to encourage growth.

Harvesting Pick fresh leaves and flowers as required. All varieties dry well as their scent and flavour become more intense. Dry in the dark at a temperature of not more than 23°C (73°F).

Propagation By cuttings, root division in spring or autumn and seed.

Pot growth Grows well in pots or window boxes if enough room is allowed for roots. Water well.

Uses To add flavour to meat dishes, sausages, most Italian dishes but particularly pizzas, salads, egg and vegetable dishes. Sweet marjoram has the most subtle taste. The dried leaves are often added to *pot-pourri*.

Petroselinum crispum
PARSLEY

Perhaps the best known and most frequently used of herbs, parsley is a biennial usually grown as an annual. Most varieties have dark green, curly leaves but some have flatter, broader leaves. Hamburg parsley (*Petroselinum sativum*) is grown for its roots. Parsley is native to the Mediterranean regions and therefore needs protection in winter in cooler climes. It is not surprising that it has been in use for over 300 years as not only does parsley improve the taste and appearance of most savoury

Don't be put off by the story that parsley will only grow for a household where a woman is the dominant partner. Given the right attention it will flourish anywhere and provide you with an instant garnish and flavouring for almost any savoury dish. Container grown plants may be brought indoors over winter.

Above and right *Dill is a large, decorative herb, reaching a height of about 90cm (3ft). It has feathery leaves, similar to those of fennel, and yellow flowers. Both the leaves and the seeds are used in cooking, particularly to flavour vinegar. The leaves can be added to salads and vegetable and fish dishes.*

dishes, but is also an important source of iron, vitamin C and iodine and eaten regularly it will improve your health.

Soil Moist but well-drained with natural or added lime.

Position Semi-shade.

Planting and cultivation Sow seeds in spring and in succession throughout the summer, watering the seedlings well. The seeds are slow to germinate, taking about five to eight weeks, although an initial soaking may help speed the process. Thin seedlings to 8cm (3in) apart and then to 20cm (8in) apart as, ideally, parsley plants should not touch each other. Weed regularly and protect from winter frosts. Flower stalks should be cut off as soon as they appear in the second year to delay the plant going to seed.

Harvesting Pick fresh as required. Parsley does not respond well to drying.

Pot growth Will grow well in pots, if they are deep enough to contain the long root. Or grow in tubs, containers or special parsley pots in a yard or patio.

Uses To make parsley sauce and butter, and chopped and sprinkled over almost every savoury dish you can think of, as well as being part of *bouquet garni*. Chewed after eating garlic, parsley will remove the smell. Made into a tisane, parsley tea acts as a diuretic.

Peucedanum graveolens (syn. *Anethum graveolens*)
DILL

Similar in appearance to fennel, dill is an annual, originally from around the Mediterranean, grown for its aromatic seeds and leaves. It has delicate, feathery, blue-green leaves, yellow flowers and grows to a height of about 90cm (3ft). It is found growing wild in the warmer parts of Europe.

Soil Well drained and of fine tilth for the seeds.

Position Sunny, but not near fennel as they might cross-pollinate one another.

Planting and cultivation Sow seeds shallowly in the spring and then successfully throughout the summer. Sow *in situ* as dill does not like being transplanted. Thin seedlings to 23cm (9in) apart and keep free from weeds.

Harvesting Pick fresh leaves as required from six weeks after sowing. Leaves for drying are best picked just before the flowers come out when the leaves are at their best. To obtain seeds, let the plant flower and allow the seeds to ripen on the plant. Shake out and store.

Propagation By seed.

Pot growth Will grow in pots and window boxes if they are deep enough.

Uses Both the leaves and seeds are used to flavour vinegar, pickles (especially cucumber), soups, fish dishes and sauces and vegetables such as cabbage and courgettes (zucchini). Use with restraint as the flavour is quite strong. The seeds contain an essential oil with carminative and stimulant properties, which is particularly associated with dill water used by mothers to wind their babies.

Pimpinella anisum
ANISE

A medium tall annual with serrated leaves and clusters of white flowers. The aromatic fruits containing the oil-bearing seed are called aniseed, and it is principally for these that anise is grown. It is native to the Middle East but is also grown in quantity in India, Greece, Spain and Egypt.

Soil Light, dry and limy.

Position Sunny and sheltered.

Although anise is native to the Mediterranean regions, *it will grow in cooler climates. The seeds, known as aniseed, were once popular as flavourings for confectionery and cakes but are now more frequently used to flavour curries, liqueurs and spirits, such as ouzo and pernod, and to make tisanes which are said to aid the digestion.*

Planting and cultivation Sow seeds in spring to allow them to produce seed to be ripened during the summer.

Harvesting The fruits will only ripen if it has been a really hot summer, when the fruit will turn greyish-green in colour. Cut the whole flower stems and hang them upside down in an airy place to continue ripening. Shake out the seeds and store them.

Propagation By seed.

Pot growth Not recommended.

Uses The seeds are used for flavouring drinks, such as Pernod, Ouzo and Anisette, biscuits (cookies), bread and cakes. Aniseed tea is reputed to be a remedy for diarrhoea and to soothe indigestion.

82

Portulaca oleracea
PURSLANE

Purslane is a half-hardy annual with a low-spreading habit. It grows principally in tropical and sub-tropical regions but will survive quite happily in cool temperate climes if planting is delayed until after the last frost. The roots of purslane are fibrous and the leaves small, ovate and fleshy. It grows to a height of about 15cm (6in) and has yellow flowers. Purslane is rich in vitamins and minerals and may be found growing wild in hot, dry climates but is also quite easy to cultivate.

Purslane is a sprawling plant with rosettes of fleshy leaves. Combined with sorrel, the leaves are an important ingredient of the French soup bonne femme. Young leaves may be used raw for salads while older, tougher leaves should be cooked in the same way as spinach or pickled in vinegar for winter use.

Soil Sandy and well drained.

Position Sunny.

Planting and cultivation Either sow seed or set out small plants in spring and sow in succession until the end of summer. Purslane plants should be thinned out to allow about 15cm (6in) between them.

Harvesting The leaves may be picked, for use fresh or to be dried, about six weeks after sowing. Pick whole shoots when they are about 8cm (3in) long.

Propagation By seed, cuttings or root division.

Pot growth Not suitable.

Uses The young leaves may be used in salads, but as they become older and more fibrous, use them in the same way as those of spinach, in soups and as a vegetable. The shoots may also be cooked and eaten as a vegetable while the leaves make a pleasant herbal tisane.

Rosmarinus officinalis
ROSEMARY

A beautiful, evergreen shrub with aromatic leaves, rosemary makes a useful small hedge. It originates from the Mediterranean region and its Latin name means 'dew of the sea'. The leaves of rosemary are leathery, needle-like in shape and grey-green in colour while the flowers are pale blue. This perennial shrub reaches a height of about 90cm (3ft) and is very attractive to bees.

Soil Sandy and well drained, it will not tolerate wet roots.

Position Sheltered and sunny, preferably against a warm wall.

Planting and cultivation It can be grown from seed but germination is so slow that it is more satisfactory to grow from rooted cuttings or bought plants. Put these out in late spring or early summer 38in (15in) apart. Prune new shoots after flowering each year. Protect young plants from frost in winter in areas where this is necessary.

Harvesting Pick fresh leaves and flowers as required, and cut shoots for drying in the summer.

Propagation Easily propagated from cuttings taken from new growth in spring or by root division. Overwinter cuttings in a greenhouse and plant out the following spring.

Pot growth Rosemary makes a good pot plant which should be brought indoors during the winter in cooler climates and clipped into a neat shape.

Uses With roast meats, particularly lamb, veal and chicken. In stuffings, marinades and egg dishes, and with fish, shellfish and vegetables. It is also good with sweeter things such as jellies and fruit drinks. It makes a good tea and the fragrant oil extracted from the leaves is used in perfumes, shampoos and other cosmetics.

Top *Purslane seed, sown in early spring, should produce a good crop, although it does require more water than other herbs. Above Rosemary is an evergreen shrub which can grow to a height of 2m (6ft) or more. It is more commonly grown from rooted cuttings or bought plants rather than seed and will thrive in the garden or indoors. Rosemary is strong and aromatic, so use it sparingly in cooking. Add it to meat, game, fish, egg and poultry dishes. It can be used to make excellent tisane.*

Rumex acetosa
SORREL

Rumex acetosa is the most common form of sorrel, although there is another variety *R. scutatus* which is particularly prized for soup-making. Both are members of the dock family and border between being a herb and a leaf vegetable. Sorrel is a hardy perennial, with hastate leaves rich in vitamin C. Cosmopolitan in its distribution, the sorrel plant grows to a height of about 60cm (2ft).

Soil Most light, well-drained soils, preferably acidic.

Position Sunny but will tolerate partial shade.

Planting and cultivation It can be raised from seed sown in spring or from

root divisions. Plant in spring or autumn. Leave 30cm (12in) between plants. Cut off the flowering stems to encourage leaf growth and prevent it going to seed. Replant bed every four years.

Harvesting Leaves may be used fresh about three months after sowing, and if sorrel plants are protected in winter, may be picked throughout the year.

Propagation By seed and root division in spring or autumn.

Pot growth Not suitable.

Uses The taste is bitter and lemony so use with discretion in cooking. Young, tender leaves may be eaten raw in salad but later treat like spinach leaves and use in soups as a puréed vegetable. A tea made from the leaves is a sharp-tasting tonic and is said to purify the blood.

There are in fact two varieties of sorrel, garden sorrel, illustrated above, and French sorrel. Both are members of the dock family and have a high vitamin C content. The leaves are used raw in salads, cooked to make a delicious soup (which has become a speciality of France) and as a vegetable dish similar to spinach.

Right Rue is a hardy, evergreen shrub with lovely, blue-green leaves and soft, yellow flowers in summer. It is now grown almost entirely for its decorative qualities and because of its long historical association with the herb garden. Far right Sage is traditionally used with all rich and fatty meats, as its strong taste counteracts greasiness.

Ruta graveolens
RUE

Rue is a highly aromatic and decorative evergreen shrub. It has lacy, blue-green leaves, small yellow flowers and grows to a height of about 60-90cm (2-3ft). Although it is native to the Mediterranean, this perennial herb will tolerate cooler climates and is an attractive hedging plant grown almost entirely for its decorative qualities.

Soil Well drained with natural or added lime.

Position Full sun.

Planting and cultivation Either sow seeds or set out plants in early spring. Prune to shape and pinch out the flower buds.

Harvesting Use leaves as required.

Propagation By seed, root division or cuttings 10-14cm (4-6in) long, taken from ripened side shoots in late summer and rooted in a cold frame to plant out the following autumn or spring.

Uses Rue is grown principally as a decorative plant. Its leaves are bitter but may be used in very small quantities to flavour salad dressings. Many centuries ago it was taken medicinally as a tisane and thought to preserve good health.

Salvia officinalis
SAGE

This fast-spreading, perennial shrub has had a reputation for centuries as a cure for all ills and an aid to longevity. There are numerous varieties of sage but the one most commonly grown in nurseries for culinary purposes does not flower in cooler climates and so cannot be raised from seed. The common or garden variety has small mauve flowers and nearly all varieties have hairy, grey-green, deeply-veined leaves. There is one particularly individual variety called pineapple sage (*Salvia rutilans*) whose leaves smell of pineapple. It has red flowers and is of no culinary use. Sage grows well around the Mediterranean and in areas with temperate climates and reaches a height of about 60cm (2ft).

Soil Dry and well drained. Sage hates wet soil.

Position Full sun.

Planting and cultivation Sow seeds, where possible, in spring and do not plant out in cooler climates until after the last frost. Otherwise set out small plants 40cm (16in) apart in well hoed and weeded soil. Prune to

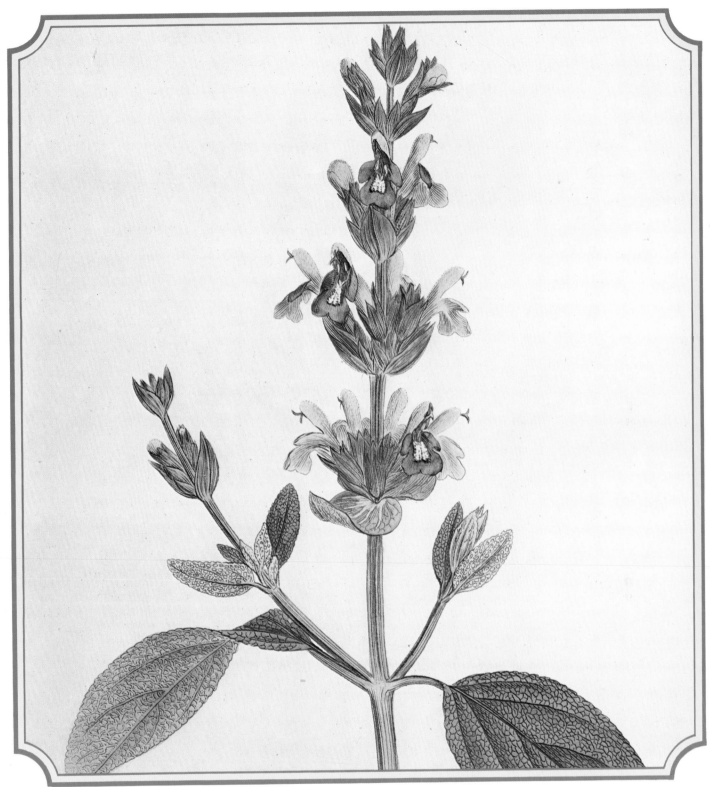

shape regularly and renew bed every four years.

Harvesting Pick leaves as required, but they are at their best just before flowering, where this occurs. Dry very slowly at a low temperature.

Propagation For layers, peg down peripheral stems, and when they have grown independent roots, cut away and transplant or take cuttings.

Pot growth Grows well in large pots, tubs and window sills. Shape regularly.

Uses Most famous in sage and onion stuffing. Particularly used with rich, fatty meats such as pork, eel and duck, but tastes equally good with veal, liver, sausages, cheese and tomato dishes. As a tisane it has been taken medicinally for centuries and also used as a mouthwash.

Sage is a small shrub which grows to a height of about 60cm (2ft). There are many different varieties of sage but the most frequently grown garden sage has narrow, grey-green leaves and blue to purple flowers. All varieties, however, have a tendency to straggle and need to be trimmed regularly to give them shape.

87

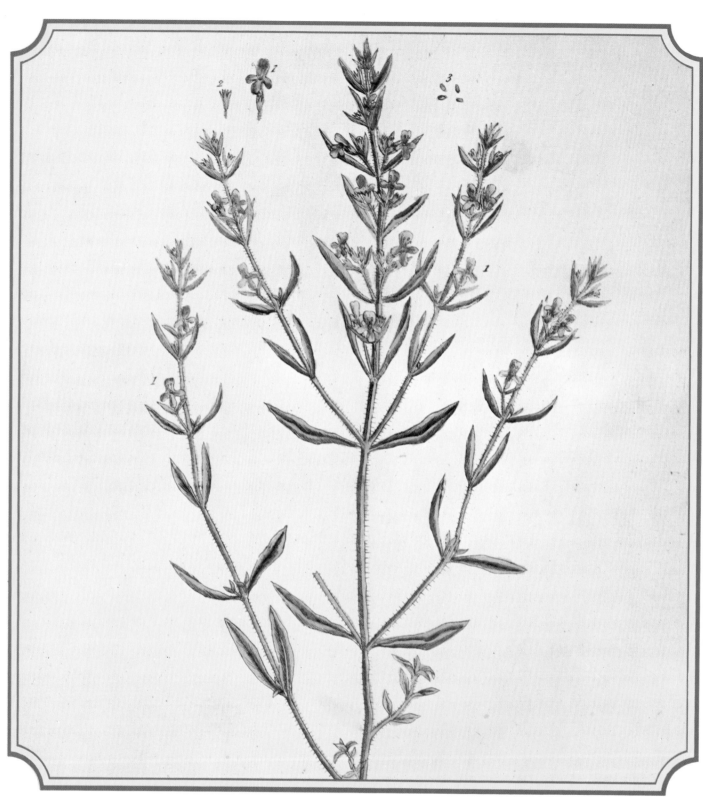

Savory is an aromatic herb of which there are two different types: summer and winter savory. Summer savory is an annual and grows to a height of about 30cm (1ft). Winter savory is a perennial plant which grows rapidly into a bushy shrub. Both types of savory have a similar spicy flavour resembling that of thyme.

Satureia hortensis
SUMMER SAVORY
Satureia montana
WINTER SAVORY

Both varieties have a similar spicy taste, although that of summer savory is subtler and more highly valued by cooks. *S. hortensis* is an annual, 30cm (12in) high with sparse, dark green, narrow leaves and white or lavender flowers. *S. montana* is a low growing, hardy perennial, 15-30cm (6-12in) high with aromatic leaves and white or blue flowers. Both savories are of Mediterranean origin and collectively are known as the 'bean herb'

Soil Good, well drained soils.

Aspect Sunny.

Planting and cultivation Sow seeds in spring, or buy and set out small plants for quicker results. Set 15cm (6in) apart. Winter savory may need protection from frost in winter.

Harvesting Cut summer savory sprigs before the plant begins to flower and use fresh or dried. Winter savory is an evergreen and may be picked sparingly throughout the winter as well as the summer.

Pot growth Both savories grow well in pots, tubs and boxes, although it is advisable to bring winter savory indoors during the winter in cooler climates.

Uses Traditionally used in all bean dishes to increase the flavour and make them more digestible. Good in stuffings and casseroles, and, chopped fresh, can be added to salads and soups. Also served with trout and pork dishes.

Symphytum officinale
COMFREY

Native to the temperate regions of Europe and Asia, comfrey has been used for centuries as a healing herb of great virtue. It is a hardy perennial, about 90cm (3ft) high, with hairy leaves and stem. The bell-shaped flowers may be coloured blue, purple, pink or cream.

Soil Damp.

Position Shady.

Planting and cultivation Sow seeds in spring but nip off flower buds as it is self-seeding and spreads quickly.

Harvesting Pick leaves during the summer and dig up roots, if required in the autumn.

Propagation By seed or root division during the autumn.

Pot growth Not suitable.

Uses Mainly medicinal; as a tisane, ointment or root poultice it is used as a cough medicine and to staunch bleeding and heal wounds. The leaves may be cooked like spinach and are good with eggs, or fresh chopped leaves can be added to salads. It is also used to make wine.

Tanacetum vulgare
TANSY

A particularly beautiful, perennial herb introduced into the garden with discretion as it spreads quickly. Tansy may also be found growing wild throughout Europe and parts of America. It grows to 60-90cm (2-3ft) tall and has aromatic, dark green, ferny leaves which can be 25cm (10in) long

Below, left Tansy is a wild herb which can be successfully cultivated. It has small, yellow flowers whcih contrast pleasingly with the intensely green leaves. The name is derived from the Greek word for immortality, although this may refer to its persistence as a plant rather than to any therapeutic quality. Below, centre Comfrey is particularly renowned for its use in medicine through which it acquired its other common name of 'knit-bone'. It was believed to mend broken bones and to heal sprains, swellings and backache. Below, right Winter savory is a hardy dwarf evergreen which is extremely useful as a flavouring in winter when most other herbs are not available. It has a rather strong flavour which goes particularly well with broad or runner (lima) beans and is frequently added to bean and pea soups.

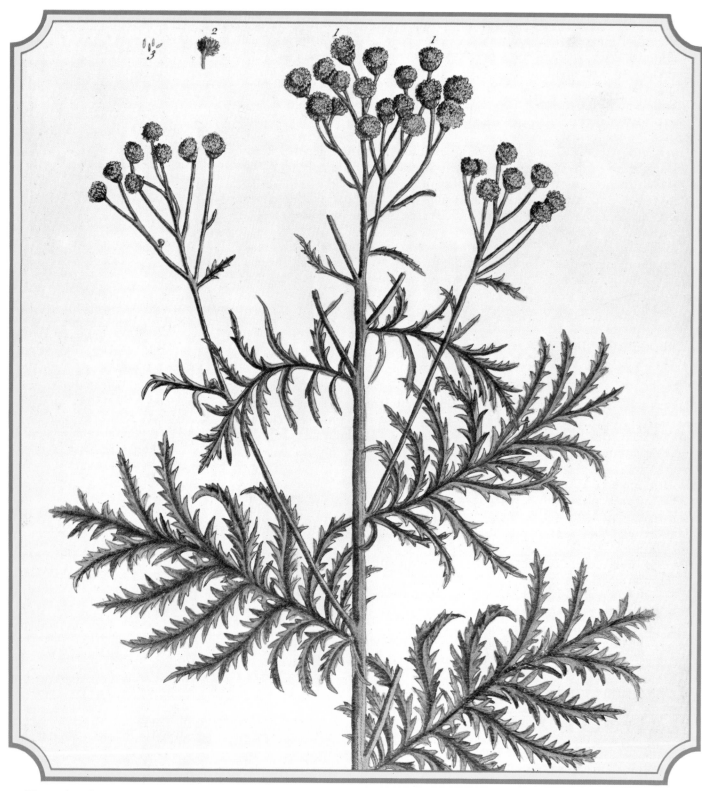

Tansy has bitter, aromatic leaves which are used in cooking to give a surprisingly pleasant flavour to desserts or savoury dishes. At one time the leaves were an important ingredient of the traditional British tansy, a confection of sugar, tansy, mint and currants enclosed in pastry and baked and eaten at Easter.

and clusters of yellow 'button' flowers.

Soil Ordinary.

Position Sunny.

Planting and cultivation Sow seed in the open in spring.

Harvesting The leaves may be harvested as required.

Propagation By seed or root division in spring or autumn.

Pot growth Not suitable.

Uses The leaves used to form an important ingredient in tansy cakes, traditionally served at Easter. The leaves were mixed with mint, sugar and currants, wrapped in pastry and baked. Tansy tea is hot and peppery and should only be taken occasionally in small quantities.

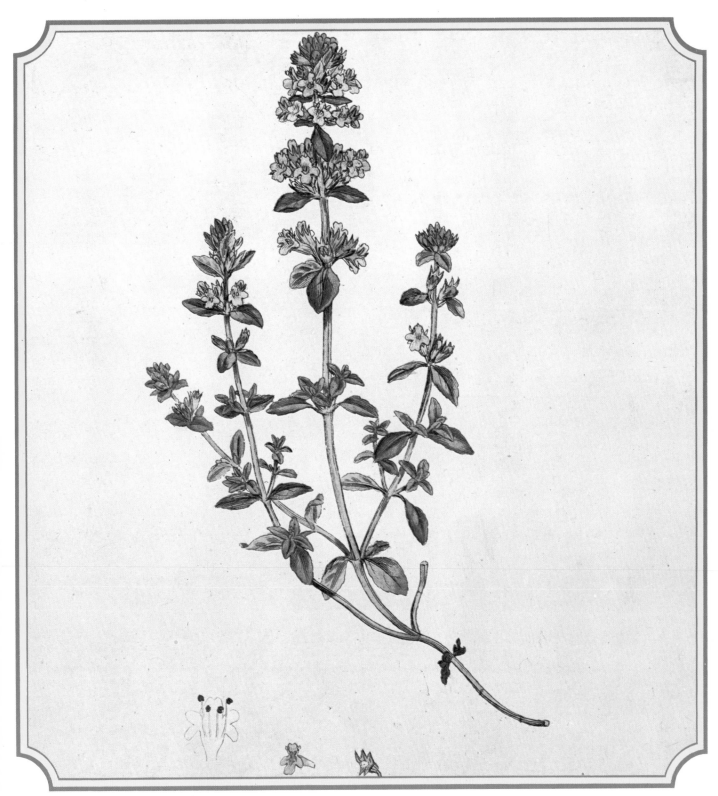

Thymus
THYME

There are numerous varieties of thyme of which the common (*T. vulgaris*) and lemon (*T. citriodorus*) are the main culinary species, although orange thyme (*T. fragantissimus*) also has a very attractive flavour. Thyme plants are perennial, grow to about 25cm (10in) tall, and are beautifully scented. Common thyme grows in the shape of a bush and has tiny, very dark leaves. Lemon thyme, along with several other varieties, is a shorter, creeping growth which spreads quickly and looks very attractive among

There are many different varieties of thyme of which the two most frequently used in cooking are common thyme and lemon thyme. Thyme is one of the three herbs that make up a bouquet garni and is particularly good in stuffings and meatball mixtures. It has a strong flavour and should be used with caution.

A nasturtium plant will add colour to your garden and flavour to your cooking. The young leaves are rich in vitamin C and give a peppery, sharp flavour to salads and cheese dishes, but use them in moderation. The flowers are lovely in salads and the green buds when pickled make a good substitute for capers.

paving stones in pathways and terraces. Thyme attracts bees.

Soil Light and well drained.

Position Full sun.

Planting and cultivation Sow seed or plant young stock in spring. Trim tops after flowering to keep plants compact. Replant every three to four years. Protect from frost in winter.

Harvesting Pick as required up to and during its flowering stage. Thyme responds well to drying.

Propagation Root division, seed or cuttings taken with a heel from the old stem. Or peg down peripheral branches and sever and transplant when independent roots have formed.

Pot growth Thyme grows well indoors in pots or in window boxes and outdoor containers.

Uses Stuffing made with a combination of common and lemon thyme is particularly good. Thyme forms part of a *bouquet garni*, and adds flavour to stews, poultry, sausages and game. Lemon thyme is good with fish or fruit dishes, and may be used dry in a *pot-pourri*. As a tisane, thyme is recommended as a cough mixture and for its digestive qualities.

Trigonella foenum graecum
FENUGREEK

A native of southern Europe and northern Africa, fenugreek should be treated as a hardy annual in temperate climates. The leaves, like those of clover, are divided into three segments and in summer the scented cream flowers produce the large pods of seeds for which the herb is grown.

Soil Well drained.

Position Sunny.

Planting and cultivation Sow seeds in spring.

Harvesting The plant is mature after about four months when it should be lifted whole and dried and the seeds shaken out.

Propagation By seed.

Pot growth Not suitable.

Uses The seeds are used in curry powders, pickles, chutneys and in the sweetmeat *halva*. Shoots from seed can be used in salad. Tisanes made from fenugreek seeds are good for the digestion. Scientists are also trying to utilise a substance found in the seed to act as an oral contraceptive.

Tropaeolum majus
NASTURTIUM

A decorative, creeping or climbing annual with bright green leaves like inverted umbrellas and brilliant flowers of yellow, orange or red. This plant originates from Peru and is rich in vitamin C.

Soil Any soil, preferably poor.

Position Sunny.

Planting and cultivation Sow seeds in spring *in situ*.

Harvesting Pick leaves and flowers as required.

Propagation By seed.

Pot growth Suitable for tubs, hanging baskets and window boxes.

Uses Apart from its purely decorative value, nasturtium buds are eaten pickled and can be substituted for capers, while the flowers and leaves can be chopped and used fresh in salads. The leaves have a hot, peppery taste so use with discretion. The roots also exude a substance which repels undesirable insects in the soil.

Top Common, or black, thyme is one of the most frequently used of culinary herbs and is is consequently the one most commonly grown. It is from this plant that thymol is extracted to be used in antiseptic gargles and mouthwashes. Above Although the nasturtium is native to Peru, it is extremely easy to cultivate in temperate climates as well. The beautiful, exotic flowers vary in shade from pale apricot to deep red and the leaves are excellent for ground cover. Many varieties can be trained to climb or trail up or down walls and trellises.

Verbena officinalis
VERVAIN

Also called 'verbena', this hardy perennial herb should not be confused with lemon verbena (*Lippa citriodora*). It has serrated, grey leaves and spikes of unscented lilac flowers in summer. Vervain was grown in herb gardens mainly because of its magical associations – it was said to ward off evil powers – although it does make a good tea.

Verbena officinalis

Vervain is grown in herb gardens mainly because of its ancient magical associations— it was used to ward off evil powers—although vervain tisane is still popular, particularly in France. It was also reputed to have medicinal properties and was frequently added to hair tonics and eye wash preparations.

Soil Rich and well drained.

Position Sunny.

Planting and cultivation Sow seeds in early spring.

Harvesting Cut sprigs in summer to use fresh, or dry before the flowers open.

Propagation Seed, cuttings and root division.

Uses A tisane made with the leaves and sweetened with honey is particularly good as a mild sedative and a remedy for digestive problems. It used to be considered as a general panacea. An infusion of the leaves used for compresses in cases of tired eyes or for inflammation of the eyelids has a cleansing and strengthening effect.

COOKING WITH HERBS

**SOUPS & STARTERS
FISH & SHELLFISH
POULTRY & GAME
VEGETABLES & SALADS
MEAT & MAIN COURSES
SAUCES, STUFFINGS & STOCKS
PUDDINGS & DESSERT
BREADS & CAKES**

SOUPS & STARTERS

Lovage soup

	Metric/UK	US
Butter	25g/1oz	2 Tbs
Medium onions, sliced	2	2
Garlic clove, crushed	1	1
Flour	25g/1oz	$\frac{1}{4}$ cup
Chicken stock	1$\frac{1}{4}$l/2 pints	5 cups
Chopped fresh lovage	2 Tbs	2 Tbs
Large potatoes, sliced	4	4
Salt and pepper		
Milk	300ml/10floz	1$\frac{1}{4}$ cups
Chopped fresh parsley	1 Tbs	1 Tbs

Melt the butter in a large saucepan. Add the onions and garlic and fry until they are soft. Remove from the heat and stir in the flour to form a smooth paste. Gradually stir in the stock and return to the heat. Bring to the boil, stirring constantly. Add the lovage, potatoes and seasoning to taste. Reduce the heat to low, cover the pan and simmer for 30 to 40 minutes, or until the potatoes are tender. Stir in the milk and bring to the boil.

Purée the soup in a blender until smooth, or rub through a strainer. Return the purée to the rinsed-out pan and reheat gently until it is hot but not boiling.

Sprinkle over the parsley and serve at once.

6 Servings

Cucumber and mint soup

	Metric/UK	US
Chicken stock	900ml/1$\frac{1}{2}$ pints	3$\frac{3}{4}$ cups
Small onion, chopped	1	1
Cucumber, thinly sliced	1	1
Mint sprigs	3	3
Cornflour (cornstarch), blended with 1$\frac{1}{2}$ Tbs water	$\frac{1}{2}$ Tbs	$\frac{1}{2}$ Tbs
Salt and pepper		

Bring the stock to the boil in a large saucepan. Reduce the heat to low and add the onion. Simmer for 10 minutes, or until it is soft. Reserve a little cucumber for garnish and add the remainder to the stock, with one mint sprig. Simmer the soup for a further 7 minutes.

Purée the mixture in a blender until smooth, or rub through a strainer. Return the purée to the rinsed-out pan and stir in the cornflour (cornstarch) mixture. Stirring constantly bring the soup to the boil, then cook for 2 to 3 minutes, or until the soup thickens and is smooth. Season to taste. Remove from the heat and set aside to cool.

Pour the soup into a large serving bowl and chill in the refrigerator until very cold. Garnish with the remaining mint sprig and reserved cucumber and serve at once.

4 Servings

Cauliflower soup

	Metric/UK	US
Large cauliflower, trimmed	1	1
Chicken stock	900ml/1$\frac{1}{2}$ pints	3$\frac{3}{4}$ cups
Salt	$\frac{1}{4}$ tsp	$\frac{1}{4}$ tsp
Butter	50g/2oz	4 Tbs
Flour	40g/1$\frac{1}{2}$oz	$\frac{1}{3}$ cup
Milk	300ml/10floz	1$\frac{1}{4}$ cups
White pepper	$\frac{1}{2}$ tsp	$\frac{1}{2}$ tsp
Ground mace	$\frac{1}{4}$ tsp	$\frac{1}{4}$ tsp
Chopped fresh chervil	1$\frac{1}{2}$ tsp	1$\frac{1}{2}$ tsp
Egg yolk	1	1
Single (light) cream	2 Tbs	2 Tbs
Lemon juice	1 tsp	1 tsp

Break the cauliflower into small flowerets. Rinse in cold water and reserve about 10 of them. Chop the remaining flowerets.

Put the stock and salt into a saucepan and bring to the boil. Add the whole flowerets and cook for about 10 minutes, or until they are tender but firm. Using a slotted spoon, transfer the flowerets to a plate. Reserve the stock.

Melt the butter in a large saucepan. Remove from the heat and stir in the flour to form a smooth paste. Gradually add the reserved stock and the milk and return to the heat. Bring to the boil, stirring constantly and cook for 2 to 3 minutes, or until the mixture thickens and is smooth. Add the chopped cauliflower, pepper, mace and chervil, and half-cover. Simmer for 15 minutes, or until the cauliflower is soft enough to be mashed. Remove the pan from the heat and rub the mixture through a strainer set over a

Refreshing and cooling, Cucumber and Mint Soup is ideal for serving on a hot summer's day.

saucepan. (Do not use a blender – the purée will be too smooth.)

Beat the egg yolk and cream together until they are lightly blended. Gradually add about 4 tablespoons of the soup purée, beating constantly. Pour the mixture very slowly into the pan, stirring constantly.

Add the reserved cauliflower flowerets to the soup and simmer gently until the soup is hot but not boiling. Do not let it come to the boil or it will curdle.

Stir in the lemon juice and serve at once.

4-6 Servings

Marigold fish and oyster soup

	Metric/UK	US
White fish, cleaned with the heads and tails left on	½kg/1lb	1lb
Onion, thinly sliced	1	1
Large carrot, thinly sliced	1	1
Bay leaf	1	1
Chopped fresh thyme	1 tsp	1 tsp
Black peppercorns, crushed	3	3
Salt	1 tsp	1 tsp
Water	1¼l/2 pints	5 cups
Beurre manié (two parts flour and one part butter blended to a paste)	50g/2oz	4 Tbs
Medium potatoes, diced	6	6
Milk	900ml/ 1½ pints	3¾ cups
Dried marigold petals	2 Tbs	2 Tbs
Fresh oysters, shelled, or canned oysters, drained	18	18

Put the fish in a large saucepan and add the vegetables, herbs, peppercorns and salt. Pour over the water and bring to the boil. Reduce the heat to low and simmer for 30 minutes, or until the fish flakes easily. Remove the pan from the heat. Pour the mixture through a fine strainer set over a bowl. Remove and discard all the bones, heads and tails from the fish and the bay leaf. Add the remaining fish flesh and vegetables to the strained stock in the bowl.

Put the stock into a blender and blend until the mixture forms a purée. Return the liquid to the rinsed-out pan and bring to the boil. Add the beurre manié, a little at a time, and cook for 2 to 3 minutes, stirring constantly, until the soup is thick and smooth.

Reduce the heat to low and add the potatoes and milk. Cook for 20 minutes, or until the potatoes are tender. Add half the marigold petals

and the oysters and simmer for 2 to 4 minutes, or until the colour from the petals has infused into the soup.

Remove the pan from the heat and transfer the soup to a warmed tureen. Sprinkle with the remaining marigold petals and serve at once.

8 Servings

Chervil and leek soup

	Metric/UK	US
Butter	75g/3oz	6 Tbs
Large leeks, washed and chopped	3	3
Medium carrot, chopped	1	1
Medium potatoes, diced	3	3
Chicken stock	1¼l/2 pints	5 cups
Salt and pepper		
Chopped fresh chervil	1 bunch	1 bunch
Single (light) cream	125ml/4floz	½ cup

Melt 50g/2oz (4 tablespoons) of butter in a large saucepan. Add the vegetables and fry for 10 minutes, stirring occasionally. Pour in the stock, then add the seasoning and chervil and bring to the boil. Reduce the heat to low, cover the pan and simmer for 40 minutes.

Purée the soup in a blender until smooth, or rub through a strainer. Return the purée to the rinsed-out pan and bring to the boil. Simmer for 5 minutes, then add the cream and remaining butter. Simmer until the butter melts. Serve at once.

6 Servings

Split pea soup with mint and tomatoes

	Metric/UK	US
Butter	25g/1oz	2 Tbs
Medium onion, chopped	1	1
Medium tomatoes, blanched, skinned, seeded and chopped	4	4
Split peas, soaked overnight and drained	225g/8oz	1 cup
Beef stock	300ml/10floz	1¼ cups
Water	300ml/10floz	1¼ cups
Salt and pepper		
Chopped fresh mint	2 Tbs	2 Tbs
Chopped fresh basil	1 tsp	1 tsp
GARNISH		
Large tomato, blanched, skinned, seeded and cut into strips	1	1
Chopped fresh mint	1 tsp	2 tsp

Melt the butter in a large saucepan. Add the onion and fry until it is soft. Add the tomatoes and peas and stir until they are well coated with the butter. Pour in the stock and water add

the seasoning, mint and basil. Bring to the boil. Reduce the heat to low, cover the pan and simmer the soup for 1½ hours, or until the peas are very soft.

Purée the mixture in a blender until smooth, or rub through a strainer. Return the purée to the rinsed-out pan and bring to the boil, stirring constantly. Garnish with the tomato strips and mint, and serve at once.

4 Servings

Celery with red caviar

An elegant and simple appetizer, Celery with Red Caviar takes only minutes to prepare. It can be accompanied, in a separate dish, by black olives.

	Metric/UK	US
Celery	2 small heads	2 small heads
Full-fat cream cheese	225g/8oz	1 cup
Chopped fresh chives	2 Tbs	2 Tbs
Chopped fresh parsley	2 Tbs	2 Tbs
Jar red caviar	90g/3½oz	3½oz
White pepper	½ tsp	½ tsp

Clean the celery and cut each stalk into three, crosswise.

Combine the cream cheese, chives, parsley, caviar and pepper until they are thoroughly blended.

Spread a little of the caviar mixture on to each celery piece and chill in the refrigerator for 30 minutes before serving.

4-6 Servings

Tarragon liver pâté

	Metric/UK	US
Butter	25g/1oz	2 Tbs
Onion, finely chopped	1	1
Lean belly of pork, minced (ground)	175g/6oz	6oz
Chicken livers, cleaned and finely chopped	½kg/1lb	1lb
Chopped fresh tarragon	2 Tbs	2 Tbs
Eggs, lightly beaten	2	2
Double (heavy) cream	2 Tbs	2 Tbs
Salt and pepper		
Ground cinnamon	½ tsp	½ tsp

Preheat the oven to cool 150°C (Gas Mark 2, 300°F).

Melt the butter in a frying-pan. Add the onion and fry until it is soft. Add the pork and fry until it is lightly browned. Add the chicken livers and fry for 5 minutes, or until they are almost cooked through. Stir in the tarragon and remove from the heat.

Rub the mixture through a strainer into a bowl, discarding any pulp

The addition of oysters and marigold petals makes Marigold Fish and Oyster Soup a colourful and luxurious first course with a delicate flavour.

Fresh mackerel cooked in wine, herbs and spices, Soused Mackerel makes an ideal supper dish for the family.

remaining in the strainer. Alternatively, purée the mixture in a blender until smooth. then add the seasoning and cinnamon.

Spoon the mixture into a lightly greased terrine or deep ovenproof dish and smooth down the top. Cover terrine or dish and place it in a deep roasting tin. Pour in enough hot water to come half way up the sides of the terrine. Put the tin into the oven and bake for 1¼ hours, or until the pâté is lightly browned and has shrunk away from the sides of the terrine. Set aside to cool completely, then chill in the refrigerator for at least 2 hours before serving. Either serve in the tin or invert over a serving plate.

4-6 Servings

Soused mackerel

	Metric/UK	US
Mackerel, filleted and rolled with the skin on the outside	8	8
Dry white wine	1l/1¾ pints	4½ cups
Carrots, sliced	2	2
Medium onions, thinly sliced	2	2
Chopped fresh marjoram	4 tsp	4 tsp
Cloves	2	2
Bay leaves	4	4
Black peppercorns	1 tsp	1 tsp
Allspice berries	1 tsp	1 tsp
Salt	1 tsp	1 tsp
Lemon, sliced	1	1
Salt	1 tsp	1 tsp
Lemon, sliced	1	1

Preheat the oven to cool 150°C (Gas Mark 2, 300°F). Place the mackerel in

a large ovenproof dish and set aside.

Put the wine, carrots and onions in a saucepan and bring to the boil. Reduce the heat to low and simmer for 10 minutes. Strain the mixture over the fish, then sprinkle over the marjoram, cloves, bay leaves, peppercorns, allspice and salt. Arrange the lemon slices around the sides of the dish.

Put the dish into the oven and bake for 1½ to 2 hours, or until the fish flakes easily. Remove from the oven and set aside to cool completely before serving.

8 Servings

Nasturtium spread
This spread can be served on crispbread or *toast as a canapé or snack, or with raw vegetables as a dip. Serve as soon as it is prepared since it will discolour if set aside for any length of time.*

	Metric/UK	US
Cream cheese	125g/4oz	½ cup
Finely chopped nasturtium leaves	2 tsp	2 tsp
Paprika	½ tsp	½ tsp
Nasturtium flowers	3	3

Put all the ingredients, except the flowers, into a bowl and beat with a wooden spoon until they are well blended.

Transfer to a serving dish and garnish with the nasturtium flowers. Serve at once.

4 Servings

FISH & SHELLFISH

Bream (porgy) with fennel and white wine

	Metric/UK	US
Bream (porgy), cleaned and gutted	1x1kg/2lb	1x2lb
Fennel sprigs	2	2
Thyme sprigs	2	2
Butter	25g/1oz	2 Tbs
Salt and pepper		
Dry white wine	150ml/5floz	⅔ cup
Olive oil	1 Tbs	1 Tbs
Fennel, sliced	1 bulb	1 bulb
Tomatoes, sliced	2	2
Lemon, thinly sliced	1	1

Preheat the oven to moderate 180°C (Gas Mark 4, 350°F).

Make two deep incisions along the back of the fish. Insert the fennel sprigs into the incisions. Divide the thyme sprigs and butter and place inside the fish, then rub them all over with salt and pepper. Arrange the fish on a rack in a large roasting pan. Pour over the wine and oil and arrange the fennel, tomato and lemon slices on top.

Put the pan into the oven and bake for about 30 minutes, or until the fish flakes easily. Baste the fish occasionally during the cooking time.

Carefully transfer the fish to a warmed serving dish and serve at once.

4 Servings

Mullet baked with rock salt

	Metric/UK	US
Rock salt	350g/12oz	2 cups
Grey mullet, cleaned but with the head left on	1x2kg/4lb	1x4lb
Chopped fresh chives	1 tsp	1 tsp
Chopped fresh tarragon	1 tsp	1 tsp
Rosemary sprig	1	1
Juice of 1 lemon		

Preheat the oven to warm 170°C (Gas Mark 3, 325°F).

Cover the bottom of a large, deep ovenproof dish with approximately one-third of the rock salt. Place the fish on the salt. Sprinkle over the chives and tarragon and arrange the rosemary sprig on top. Sprinkle over the lemon juice. Pour in the remaining rock salt to surround and cover the fish completely. With the back of a wooden spoon, pat down the salt.

Put the dish into the oven and bake the fish for 50 minutes. Remove from the oven. Using a rolling pin or pestle, break the hardened crust of the salt. Prise off with a sharp knife and discard.

Serve the fish at once, from the dish.

4 Servings

Grilled (broiled) salmon with herb butter

	Metric/UK	US
HERB BUTTER		
Chopped fresh chervil	1 Tbs	1 Tbs
Chopped fresh tarragon	1 Tbs	1 Tbs
Chopped fresh parsley	1 Tbs	1 Tbs
Chopped spinach	1 Tbs	1 Tbs
Chopped watercress	1 Tbs	1 Tbs
Anchovy fillets	8	8
Capers	2 Tbs	2 Tbs
Small gherkins	4	4
Hard-boiled egg yolks	4	4
Butter	125g/4oz	8 Tbs
Olive oil	50ml/2floz	4 Tbs
Tarragon vinegar	4 Tbs	4 Tbs
Salt and pepper		
SALMON		
Thick salmon steaks	4	4
Butter, melted	75g/3oz	6 Tbs
Salt and pepper		
Lemon, sliced	1	1
Parsley sprigs (to garnish)		

To make the butter, half-fill a saucepan with water and bring to the boil. Add the herbs, spinach and watercress and boil for 1 minutes. Drain, then pat dry on paper towels. Put into a large mortar, with the anchovy fillets, capers, gherkins and egg yolks. Pound together for 5 minutes.

Beat the butter with a wooden spoon until it is soft and creamy. Blend in the herb mixture. Put the mixture into a strainer set over a bowl and press through with the back of a wooden spoon. Gradually add the olive oil, stirring constantly. Stir in the vinegar and season to taste. Alternatively, put all the ingredients except the butter in a blender and blend until completely smooth. Transfer to a bowl and beat in the butter. Spoon the herb butter into a sauceboat and set aside.

Preheat the grill (broiler) to high.

Dry the salmon steaks with paper towels and arrange them on a rack in a lined grill (broiler) pan. Brush the melted butter over both sides of the steaks. Grill (broil) for 3 minutes on each side. Baste with any remaining melted butter and sprinkle with salt and pepper to taste. Grill (broil) for a further 3 minutes on one side, then turn over and grill (broil) them for 5 minutes more, basting once with the melted butter. If the steaks look as if they are drying out, reduce the grill (broiler) to moderate.

Transfer the salmon steaks to a warmed serving dish and garnish with lemon slices and parsley sprigs. Serve at once, with the herb butter.

4 Servings

Perch with oregano

	Metric/UK	US
Perch, filleted	1kg/2lb	2lb
Butter	25g/1oz	2 Tbs
Chopped fresh oregano	1 Tbs	1 Tbs
Salt	1 tsp	1 tsp
Red pepper flakes	$\frac{1}{4}$ tsp	$\frac{1}{4}$ tsp
Chopped fresh parsley	2 Tbs	2 Tbs
Lemon slices	4	4

Preheat the grill (broiler) to high.

Lay the fillets in a lined grill (broiler) pan. Melt the butter in a small saucepan. Stir in the oregano, salt and pepper flakes and remove from the heat. Pour the mixture over the fillets and grill (broil) the fillets for 5 minutes. Turn over and cook for a further 5

Simple and quick to prepare, Perch with Oregano tastes quite delicious.

minutes, or until the fish flakes easily. Remove from the heat.

Transfer the fillets to a warmed serving dish. Pour the cooking liquid over the fillets, sprinkle over the parsley and garnish with the lemon slices. Serve at once.

6 Servings

Provençal scallops

	Metric/UK	US
Scallops, cut into 1cm/½in pieces	700g/1½lb	1½lb
Juice of ½ lemon		
Salt and pepper		
Flour	50g/2oz	½ cup
Vegetable oil	75ml/3floz	⅓ cup
Shallots, finely chopped	3	3
Garlic cloves, crushed	3	3
Finely chopped fresh basil	1 tsp	1 tsp
Butter	25g/1oz	2 Tbs
Chopped fresh parsley	1 Tbs	1 Tbs

Gently rub the scallops with the lemon juice and salt and pepper to taste. Coat the scallops in the flour, shaking off any excess.

Heat half the oil in a large frying-pan. (The oil should cover the bottom of the pan in a thin layer so if necessary add the rest.) Add the scallops and cook for 5 minutes, or until they are evenly browned. Add the shallots, garlic and basil and cook for 2 minutes, stirring frequently. Remove from the heat and stir in the butter and parsley until the butter melts.

Serve at once.

4 Servings

Eels in herb sauce

	Metric/UK	US
Butter	75g/3oz	6 Tbs
Spinach, chopped	225g/8oz	2 cups
Chopped fresh tarragon	1 tsp	1 tsp
Chopped fresh parsley	3 Tbs	3 Tbs
Chopped fresh sage	1 tsp	1 tsp
Eels, skinned, cleaned and cut into 8cm/3in pieces	1kg/2lb	2lb

Provencal Scallops is a superb dish of scallops sautéed with garlic, basil and parsley.

104

	Metric/UK	US
Salt and pepper		
Dry white wine	300ml/ 10floz	1¼ cups
Egg yolks, lightly beaten	3	3
Lemon juice	1 Tbs	1 Tbs

Melt the butter in a large, deep frying-pan. Add the spinach and herbs and fry for 2 minutes, stirring constantly. Add the eel pieces and seasoning, then pour over the wine. Bring to the boil, reduce the heat to low and cover the pan. Simmer for 15 minutes, or until the eel is cooked through and tender. Remove the pan from the heat.

Gradually add about 4 tablespoons of the pan liquid to the egg yolks, beating constantly. Pour the egg mixture very slowly into the frying-pan, stirring constantly. Add the lemon juice and adjust the seasoning. Set aside until cool, transfer the eels to a serving dish, then chill in the refrigerator until very cold.

6 Servings

Trout with rosemary

	Metric/UK	US
Trout, cleaned	4	4
Salt and pepper		
Garlic cloves, halved	2	2
Rosemary sprigs	4	4
Olive oil	3 Tbs	3 Tbs
Lemon, cut into 8	1	1

Preheat the grill (broiler) to moderate.

Rub the fish all over with salt and pepper. Put half a garlic clove and a rosemary sprig into the cavity of each fish. Make three shallow incisions along each side of each fish and arrange them in the grill (broiler) pan.

Lightly coat the trout with the oil, then grill (broil) for 5 minutes. Turn the fish over, brush with the remaining oil and grill (broil) for a further 5 to 6 minutes, or until the fish flakes easily.

Transfer the fish to a warmed serving dish. Remove and discard the garlic and rosemary and garnish with the lemon wedges. Serve at once.

4 Servings

Eels in Herbs Sauce is a Flemish dish of eels simmered in wine and green herbs. Although it is occasionally eaten hot, it is preferable to serve this dish when it is cold. Fresh herbs should be used whenever possible and such herbs as sorrel and chervil can be included, when available, and fresh, tender nettles substituted for the spinach.

Moules marinières
(Mussels with White Wine Sauce)

Serve Moules Marinières in deep soup bowls with a fork to eat the mussels and a soup spoon for the juices.

	Metric/UK	US
Mussels	3½l/3 quarts	4 quarts
Butter	50g/2oz	4 Tbs
Small onion, finely chopped	1	1
Garlic clove, crushed	1	1
Bouquet garni	1	1
Dry white wine	450ml/15floz	2 cups
Salt and pepper		
Chopped fresh parsley	2 Tbs	2 Tbs

Wash the mussels in cold water and scrub to remove any mud and tufts. Discard any that are not tightly shut or do not close when sharply tapped. Put the mussels into a bowl of cold water and soak for 1 hour. Drain and set aside.

Melt the butter in a large saucepan. Add the onion and garlic and fry until they are soft. Add the bouquet garni, wine and seasoning and bring to the boil. Reduce the heat to low and add the mussels. Simmer, shaking the pan occasionally, for 6 to 10 minutes, or until the shells open. Using a slotted spoon, transfer the mussels to a warmed serving dish. Set aside and keep hot.

Strain the cooking liquid into a bowl, then return to the rinsed pan. Bring to the boil and boil briskly for 2 minutes. Pour over the mussels, sprinkle over the parsley and serve at once.

4 Servings

Parsley and fish pie

	Metric/UK	US
Puff pastry, chilled	350g/12oz	3 cups
Egg yolk	1	1
FILLING		
Milk	300ml/10floz	1¼ cups
Shallot, sliced	1	1
Chopped fresh marjoram	1 tsp	1 tsp
Chopped fresh dill	1 tsp	1 tsp
Bay leaf	1	1
Salt and pepper		
Butter	25g/1oz	2 Tbs
Flour	25g/1oz	¼ cup
Cod fillets, cooked, skinned and flaked	½kg/1lb	1lb
Chopped fresh parsley	8 Tbs	8 Tbs
Lemon juice	1 tsp	1 tsp

Preheat the oven to fairly hot 190°C (Gas Mark 5, 375°F).

To make the filling, put the milk, shallot, herbs and seasoning into a

saucepan and set over low heat. Infuse the milk for 10 minutes. Remove from the heat and strain into a bowl. Discard the contents of the strainer.

Melt the butter in a saucepan. Remove the pan from the heat and stir in the flour to form a smooth paste. Gradually stir in the strained milk and return the pan to the heat. Cook, stirring constantly, for 2 to 3 minutes, or until the sauce is thick and smooth. Remove from the heat and stir in the fish, parsley and lemon juice. Set aside while you roll out the pastry.

Roll out the pastry dough on a lightly floured surface to a square approximately ½cm/¼in thick. Trim the edges to straighten if necessary, then moisten the edges with a little cold water. Carefully arrange the square over a well-greased baking sheet. Spoon the fish filling into the centre of the dough. Lift each of the four corners of the dough up and over the filling until they meet in the centre. Pinch the points of the corners together to seal.

Brush the top of the pie with the egg yolk and put the sheet into the oven. Bake for 30 to 40 minutes, or until the pastry is golden brown. Remove from the oven, transfer the pie to a warmed serving dish, and serve at once.

4 Servings

Above Cod fillets folded into a creamy sauce flavoured with parsley and enveloped in a light puff pastry, Parsley and Fish Pie makes an excellent supper dish for the family. Opposite page Moules Marinière is generally served in a soup bowl, with a soup spoon for the juices, although the mussels themselves are eaten with the fingers. A good idea is to provide each person with a plate on which to put discarded shells and a bowl of water in which to rinse the fingers after eating.

POULTRY & GAME

Roast chicken with tarragon

	Metric/UK	US
Butter, softened	125g/4oz	8 Tbs
Salt and pepper		
Tarragon sprigs,		
finely chopped	6	6
Chicken	1x2½kg/5lb	1x5lb

Preheat the oven to fairly hot 190°C (Gas Mark 5, 375°F).

Beat half the butter with a wooden spoon until it is soft and creamy. Beat in salt and pepper to taste and the tarragon until thoroughly blended. Stuff the mixture into the cavity of the chicken.

Rub half the remaining butter over the breast of the chicken and place the bird, on its side, in a roasting pan. Put the pan into the oven and roast for 30 minutes. Turn the chicken on to its other side and add the remaining butter. Roast for a further 30 minutes, Reduce the oven temperature to moderate 180°C (Gas Mark 4, 350°F).

Turn the chicken on to its back and baste well with the melted butter in the pan. Roast for a final 30 minutes, basting once more, or until the chicken is cooked through and tender.

Remove from the oven and serve at once, with the pan juices.

6 Servings

Chicken with basil

	Metric/UK	US
Chicken breasts	2	2
Salt and pepper		
Butter	5g/2oz	4 Tbs
Dry white wine	125ml/4floz	½ cup
Chicken stock	125ml/4floz	½ cup
Chopped fresh basil	2 tsp	2 tsp
Beurre manié (two parts flour and one part butter blended to a paste)	2 tsp	2 tsp

Rub the chicken breasts all over with salt and pepper.

Chicken with Basil is a simple and economical dish. Serve with stuffed tomatoes and new potatoes for an appetizing lunch or dinner.

Melt the butter in a large saucepan. Add the chicken breasts and fry for about 10 minutes, or until they are evenly browned on both sides. Reduce the heat to low, cover the pan and cook for 20 to 25 minutes, or until the breasts are cooked through and tender. Using tongs, transfer the chicken to a warmed serving dish. Keep hot while you finish the sauce.

Skim any fat from the surface of the pan liquid. Add the wine, stock and basil and bring to the boil. Boil for about 10 minutes, or until the liquid has reduced by about half. Add the beurre manié, a little at a time, and cook until the sauce thickens and is smooth.

Pour the sauce over the chicken and serve at once.

2 Servings

Chicken casserole

	Metric/UK	US
Chicken pieces	4	4
Carrots, chopped	2	2
Garlic cloves, crushed	2	2
Chopped fresh parsley	2 tsp	2 tsp
Chopped fresh savory	2 tsp	2 tsp
Salt	1½ tsp	1½ tsp
Water	900ml/	
	1½ pints	3¾ cups
SAUCE		
Butter	25g/1oz	2 Tbs
Mushrooms, sliced	125g/4oz	1 cup
Chopped fresh savory	1 tsp	1 tsp
Chopped fresh parsley	½ tsp	½ tsp
Flour	25g/1oz	¼ cup
Dry white wine	125ml/4floz	½ cup
Sour cream	2 Tbs	2 Tbs

Put the chicken pieces, carrots, garlic, herbs, salt and water into a large saucepan and bring to the boil. Reduce the heat to low, cover the pan and simmer for 40 to 45 minutes, or until the chicken is cooked through and tender. Using tongs, remove the chicken from the pan. Strain and reserve the stock. When the chicken is cool enough to handle, remove and discard the skin and bones and set the meat aside.

Meanwhile, to make the sauce, melt the butter in a deep frying-pan. Add the mushrooms and herbs and fry for 3 minutes, stirring constantly. Remove the pan from the heat and stir in the flour to form a smooth paste. Gradually stir in the reserved stock and wine and return to the heat. Bring to the boil, then cook for 2 to 3 minutes, stirring constantly, or until the sauce thickens and is smooth.

Return the chicken pieces to the pan and baste well with the sauce. Simmer for a further 2 minutes to reheat the chicken, then remove from the heat. Stir in the sour cream and transfer the mixture to a warmed serving dish. Serve at once.

4 Servings

Chicken with rosemary

	Metric/UK	US
Large chicken quarters	4	4
Salt and pepper		
Butter	75g/3oz	6 Tbs
Large onions, thinly sliced	2	2
Orange juice	450ml/	
	15floz	2 cups
Chopped fresh rosemary	1 Tbs	1 Tbs
Grated orange rind	1 Tbs	1 Tbs
Cornflour (cornstarch), blended with 1 Tbs water	1½ Tbs	1½ Tbs

Rub the chicken pieces all over with salt and pepper.

Melt two-thirds of the butter in a large saucepan. Add the chicken pieces and fry until they are deeply and evenly browned. Using tongs, transfer them to a plate. Melt the remaining butter in the pan. Add the onions and fry until they are soft. Pour over the orange juice and bring to the boil, stirring occasionally. Stir in the rosemary and orange rind.

Reduce the heat to low and return the chicken pieces to the pan. Baste well with the juice. Cover and simmer for 40 minutes, or until the chicken is cooked through and tender. Using tongs, transfer the chicken to a warmed serving dish. Keep hot while you finish the sauce.

Bring the pan liquid to the boil and boil briskly for 3 minutes, or until it has reduced slightly. Reduce the heat to low and stir in the cornflour (cornstarch) mixture. Cook for 2 to 3 minutes, stirring constantly, or until the sauce is thick and smooth. Pour over the chicken and serve at once.

4 Servings

Rosemary is an evergreen shrub of Mediterranean origin whose leaves are used to flavour meat, especially lamb, and breads as well as poultry.

Marinated overnight in a mixture of yogurt, herbs and spices, Indian Chicken Kebabs are delicious served with naan bread, salad and a variety of chutneys.

Chicken Kiev

	Metric/UK	US
Butter	125g/4oz	8 Tbs
Chopped fresh parsley	1 Tbs	1 Tbs
Chopped fresh chives	1 Tbs	1 Tbs
Garlic cloves, crushed	2	2
Salt and pepper to taste		
Chicken breasts, skinned and boned	8	8
Flour	50g/2oz	½ cup
Eggs, lightly beaten	2	2
Dry breadcrumbs	175g/6oz	2 cups
Sufficient vegetable oil for deep-frying		

Beat the butter with a wooden spoon until it is soft and creamy. Beat in the parsley, chives, garlic and season to taste with salt and pepper. Divide the butter mixture into eight pieces, then shape them into small cigar shapes. Chill the shapes in the refrigerator until they are firm.

Place each chicken breast between two sheets of greaseproof or waxed paper and pound until it is thin. Remove the greaseproof or waxed paper and wrap each breast around a piece of the butter mixture, envelope fashion, so that the butter is completely enclosed.

Dip the chicken parcels, first in the flour, then in the eggs and finally in the breadcrumbs, coating them completely and shaking off any excess. Chill the pieces in the refrigerator for 1 hour.

Heat the oil in a deep-frying pan until it reaches 185°C (360°F) on a deep-fat thermometer, or until a small cube of stale bread dropped into the oil turns golden in 55 seconds. Carefully arrange the breasts, two or three at a time, in a deep-frying basket and lower them into the oil. Fry for 5 to 6 minutes, or until they are golden brown and crisp. Remove from the oil, drain on paper towels and keep warm while you fry the remaining pieces.

Serve hot.

4 Servings

Indian chicken kebabs

	Metric/UK	US
Yogurt	150ml/5floz	⅔ cup
Garlic cloves, crushed	4	4
Fresh root ginger, peeled and chopped	4cm/1½in piece	1½in piece
Small onion, grated	1	1
Hot chilli powder	1½ tsp	1½ tsp
Ground coriander	1 Tbs	1 Tbs
Salt	1 tsp	1 tsp
Chicken breasts, skinned and boned	4	4
GARNISH		
Large onion, thinly sliced into rings	1	1
Large tomatoes, thinly sliced	2	2
Chopped fresh coriander leaves	2 Tbs	2 Tbs

Put the yogurt, garlic, ginger, onion, chilli powder, coriander and salt into a bowl and beat well to blend. Set aside.

Cut the chicken meat into 2½cm/1in cubes and add to the yogurt mixture, basting thoroughly. Cover the bowl and put into the refrigerator. Leave for at least 6 hours, or overnight.

Preheat the grill (broiler) to high.

Thread the chicken cubes on to skewers and arrange on a rack in a lined grill (broiler) pan. Cook for 5 to 6 minutes, turning occasionally, or until the cubes are cooked through and tender.

Remove the skewers from the heat and slide the kebabs on to a warmed serving dish. Garnish with the onion rings, tomato slices and chopped coriander leaves. Serve at once.

4 Servings

Matzo chicken with dill

	Metric/UK	US
Eggs, lightly beaten	8	8
Medium onion, finely chopped	1	1
Chopped fresh dill	6 Tbs	6 Tbs
Chopped fresh parsley	4 Tbs	4 Tbs
Salt	2 tsp	2 tsp
Black pepper	1 tsp	1 tsp
Ground mace	½ tsp	½ tsp
Cooked chicken meat, cut into strips	½kg/1lb	1lb
Mushrooms, finely chopped	225g/8oz	2 cups
Butter	50g/2oz	4 Tbs
Matzos	5	5
Chicken stock	450ml/15floz	2 cups

Preheat the oven to fairly hot 190°C (Gas Mark 5, 375°F).

Beat the eggs, onion, dill, 3 tablespoons of parsley, seasoning and mace until they are light and frothy. Add the chicken and mushrooms and mix well. Set aside.

Melt the butter in a small saucepan. Remove the pan from the heat and pour about ½ tablespoon of the melted butter into a 23cm/9in square baking tin or dish. Tip and rotate the dish to cover evenly. Reserve the remaining butter.

Soak the matzos in the chicken stock for 1 minutes. Remove from the dish and set aside. Discard the stock.

Put one matzo on the bottom of the prepared dish and cover with about a quarter of the chicken mixture. Top with another matzo. Repeat these layers until the ingredients are used up, ending with a layer of matzo. Pour over the reserved butter and remaining parsley.

Put the dish into the oven and bake for 30 minutes, or until the top is browned. Remove from the oven and serve at once.

4-6 Servings

Duck with sauerkraut

	Metric/UK	US
Duck	1x2¾kg/6lb	1x6lb
Salt and pepper		
Butter	75g/3oz	6 Tbs
Canned sauerkraut, drained and rinsed	1kg/2lb	2lb
Salt pork, diced	50g/2oz	⅓ cup
Vegetable oil	50ml/2floz	¼ cup
Medium onions, thinly sliced	2	2
Medium carrots, thinly sliced	2	2
Cooking apple, peeled, cored and chopped	1	1
Dry white wine	250ml/8floz	1 cup
Chicken stock	175ml/6floz	¾ cup
Garlic clove	1	1
Peppercorns	6	6
Parsley sprigs	4	4
Bay leaf	1	1
Juniper berries	10	10

Preheat the oven to warm 170°C (Gas Mark 3, 325°F).

Prepare the duck by clipping the wing ends and neck and trussing so that the wings and legs are close to the body. Prick the skin around the thighs, back and lower breast. Rub salt and pepper into the cavity, then close with a skewer.

Melt the butter in a large flameproof casserole. Add the duck and fry until it

Opposite page, above, *Crisp,
golden pastry enclosing a creamy
herb-flavoured filling, Turkey and
Walnut Pie is a delectable way of
using up leftover cooked turkey.
Opposite page, below Stuffed
Roast Goose filled with a juicy
and aromatic combination of
parsley, thyme and apples is the
ideal dish for a large dinner party.*

is evenly browned. Cover the casserole
and put into the oven. Braise for 2
hours, or until the duck is cooked
through and tender.

After the duck has been cooking for
about 1 hour, prepare the sauerkraut.
Blanch the salt pork in water for about
5 minutes to remove the excess salt.
Drain and dry thoroughly on paper
towels.

Heat the oil in a large, deep frying-
pan. Add the salt pork and fry until it
resembles small croûtons and has
rendered most of its fat. Add the
onions and carrots and fry until they
are soft. Add the apple and sauerkraut
and stir well. Pour in the wine and
stock and bring to the boil. Tie all the
remaining ingredients together in a
small cheesecloth bag and put into the
middle of the sauerkraut mixture.
Reduce the heat to low, cover the pan
and simmer the sauerkraut for 30 to
40 minutes. Remove the cheesecloth
bag at the end of the period. Remove
the juniper berries from the bag and
return them to the sauerkraut. Discard
the remaining contents of the bag.
Season to taste.

When the duck is cooked, transfer it
to a warmed serving dish. Untruss.
Surround the duck with the sauerkraut
mixture and serve at once.

4 Servings

Stuffed roast goose

	Metric/UK	US
Oven-ready goose	1x3½kg/8lb	1x8lb
Lemon, quartered	1	1
Salt and pepper		
STUFFING		
Fresh white breadcrumbs	350g/12oz	6 cups
Finely grated rind and juice of 3 lemons		
Finely chopped fresh parsley	10 Tbs	10 Tbs
Finely chopped fresh lemon thyme	1½ tsp	1½ tsp
Salt and pepper		
Cooking apples, peeled, cored and grated	2	2
Eggs, lightly beaten	3	3
Butter, melted	40g/1½oz	3 Tbs
Cider	300ml/10floz	1¼ cups

Preheat the oven to very hot 230°C
(Gas Mark 8, 450°F).

Prick the goose all over with a fork.
Rub the skin with three of the lemon
quarters. Squeeze the juice of the
remaining quarter into the cavity. Rub
the skin all over with salt and pepper
and set the goose aside.

To make the stuffing, beat the
breadcrumbs, lemon rind and juice,
herbs, seasoning and apples together.
Then add the eggs, melted butter and
cider until the mixture is smooth and
thick. Spoon the stuffing into the
cavity of the goose and secure the
opening with a skewer or a trussing
needle and thread.

Arrange the goose, on its breast, on
a rack in a roasting pan. Place the pan
in the oven and roast for 15 minutes.
Reduce the oven temperature to
moderate 180°C (Gas Mark 4, 350°F)
and roast for a further 2½ to 3 hours,
or until the bird is cooked through and
tender, removing the fat frequently
from the pan. Turn the goose on to its
back halfway through the cooking
period.

Remove the goose from the oven
and remove and discard the skewer or
trussing thread. Serve at once.

8 Servings

Turkey and walnut pie

	Metric/UK	US
Butter	25g/1oz	2 Tbs
Mushrooms, sliced	225g/8oz	2 cups
Flour	25g/1oz	¼ cup
Salt and pepper		
Double (heavy) cream	300ml/10floz	1¼ cups
Sour cream	150ml/5floz	⅔ cup
Chopped fresh thyme	1 tsp	1 tsp
Chopped fresh sage	1 tsp	1 tsp
Bay leaf	1	1
Cooked turkey, cubed	700g/1½lb	1½lb
Walnuts, chopped	125g/4oz	⅔ cup
Puff pastry, chilled	375g/12oz	3 cups
Egg yolk	1	1

Preheat the oven to hot 220°C (Gas
Mark 7, 425°F).

Melt the butter in a saucepan and
add the mushrooms. Cook, stirring
frequently, for 3 minutes.

Remove the pan from the heat and
transfer the mushrooms to a plate. Stir
the flour, salt and pepper into the pan
juices to make a smooth paste. Gradually add the double (heavy) cream and
sour cream, stirring constantly. Stir in
the thyme, sage and bay leaf.

Return the pan to the heat and cook,
stirring constantly, for 10 minutes.
Remove and discard the bay leaf.
Return the mushrooms to the pan and
add the turkey and walnuts. Spoon the
mixture into a deep pie dish and
set aside.

Roll out the dough to about ½cm/¼in
thick. Cut off a strip of dough about
1cm/½in wide, long enough to fit the
rim of the pie dish. Moisten the rim

with a little water and press down the dough strip. Moisten the strip with water.

Lift the remaining dough on to the rolling pin, and lay it over the pie dish. Trim and crimp the edges to seal. Make a small slit in the centre of the dough. Brush the top with the egg yolk.

Place the pie in the oven and bake for 50 minutes. Reduce the temperature to fairly hot 190°C (Gas Mark 5, 375°F) and continue baking for 35 minutes or until the pastry is golden brown. Remove the pie from the oven and serve immediately.

4-6 Servings

Partridge pot roast

	Metric/UK	US
Butter	50g/2oz	4 Tbs
Medium onions, chopped	2	2
Carrots, sliced	2	2
Streaky (fatty) bacon slices, chopped	6	6
Mushrooms, sliced	125g/4oz	1 cup
Partridges, trussed and larded	4	4
Salt and pepper		
Bouquet garni	1	1
Beef stock	900ml/1½pts	3¾ cups
Red wine	125ml/4floz	½ cup
Chopped fresh parsley	2 Tbs	2 Tbs

Melt the butter in a large frying-pan. Add the onions and carrots and fry until the onions are soft. Transfer the vegetables to a large flameproof casserole. Add the bacon and mushrooms to the pan and fry until the bacon is crisp and has rendered most of its fat. Transfer the bacon mixture to the casserole.

Place the partridges in the pan and cook, turning them occasionally, for 8 to 10 minutes or until they are lightly and evenly browned. Add the partridges to the casserole along with the salt, pepper and bouquet garni. Pour over the stock and wine. Place the casserole over high heat and bring the liquid to the boil. Reduce the heat to low, cover and cook, stirring occasionally, for 1 hour or until the partridges are tender and cooked through.

Remove the partridges from the casserole, cut each one into 4 pieces and keep hot while you make the sauce.

Strain the cooking liquid and set the vegetables aside to keep warm. Remove and discard the bouquet garni.

Return the cooking liquid to the casserole. Bring to the boil and keep at the boil for about 8 minutes or until the liquid has reduced by about 1 third. Return the partridges and vegetables to the casserole and stir in the parsley. Simmer for a few minutes until the partridges are heated through. Serve immediately.

4 Servings

Venison pie

	Metric/UK	US
Boned lean venison, cubed	700g/1½lb	1½lb
Lambs' kidneys, skinned, cored and chopped	225g/8oz	8oz
Salt and pepper		
Mixed spice or ground allspice	1 tsp	1 tsp
Ground mace	¼ tsp	¼ tsp
Large onion, finely chopped	1	1
Chopped fresh parsley	2 Tbs	2 Tbs
Beef stock	250ml/8floz	1 cup
Puff pastry, chilled	175g/6oz	1½ cups
Red wine	50ml/2floz	¼ cup
Red wine vinegar	1 Tbs	1 Tbs
Olive oil	2 Tbs	2 Tbs
Egg yolk, lightly beaten	1	1

Put the meats, seasoning, spices, onion and parsley into a large saucepan and pour over the stock. Bring to the boil. Reduce the heat to low, cover the pan and simmer for 2 hours. Remove the pan from the heat and set aside to cool completely. When the mixture is cold, skim any fat from the surface.

Preheat the oven to very hot 230°C (Gas Mark 8, 450°F).

Roll out the pastry dough on a lightly floured surface to a 25cm/10in diameter circle. Cut a strip from outside the circle, about 2½cm/1in wide.

Using a slotted spoon, transfer the venison and kidneys to a 23cm/9in pie dish and pour in 75ml/3floz (⅓ cup) of the cooking liquid, the wine, vinegar and oil. Discard the remaining cooking liquid. Put a pie funnel in the middle of the dish. Press the thin dough strip around the rim of the pie dish and moisten with water. Lift the dough circle on to the pie dish and press the edges together to seal. Brush the dough with the beaten egg yolk.

Put the dish into the oven and bake for 10 minutes. Reduce the oven temperature to moderate 180°C (Gas Mark 4, 350°F) and bake for a further 20 to 25 minutes, or until the pastry is golden brown.

Remove from the oven and serve at once.

6 Servings

A traditional British dish, Venison Pie tastes delicious. The meat is first simmered in stock, and then enclosed in puff pastry. Serve with new potatoes boiled with mint for a delicious and nourishing meal.

MEAT & MAIN COURSES

Marinated beef and pot roast

	Metric/UK	US
Rump steak, rolled and tied	1x2¾kg/6lb	1x6lb
Dry red wine	600ml/1 pint	2½ cups
Medium onion, thinly sliced into rings	1	1
Garlic cloves	4	4
Finely chopped fresh basil	2 tsp	2 tsp
Finely chopped fresh oregano	1 tsp	1 tsp
Butter	25g/1oz	2 Tbs
Olive oil	50ml/2floz	¼ cup
Salt and pepper		
Canned peeled tomatoes, drained	425g/14oz	14oz
Black olives, stoned (pitted)	50g/2oz	½ cup
Beurre manié (two parts flour and one part butter blended to a paste)	1 Tbs	1 Tbs
Chopped fresh parsley	1 Tbs	1 Tbs

Put the meat into a large bowl. Add the wine, onion, garlic, basil and oregano, and stir well. Set aside at room temperature for 6 hours, basting occasionally.

Preheat the oven to moderate 180°C (Gas Mark 4, 350°F).

Remove the meat from the marinade and dry on paper towels. Reserve the marinade.

Melt the butter with the oil in a large flameproof casserole. Add the meat and fry until it is evenly browned. Add the reserved marinade and season to taste. Bring to the boil. Remove the casserole from the heat and transfer it to the oven. Braise for 1½ hours. Add the tomatoes and braise for a further 1 hour, or until the meat is cooked through and tender.

Remove the casserole from the oven. Using two large forks, transfer the meat to a carving board. Cut into thick slices, arrange them on a warmed serving dish and keep hot while you finish the sauce.

Skim off any fat from the surface of the cooking liquid, then strain into a bowl, pressing down on the vegetables with the back of a wooden spoon to extract all the liquid. Return the strained liquid to the casserole. Set the casserole over high heat and bring to the boil. Add the olives. Reduce the heat to low and add the beurre manié, a little at a time, and cook until the liquid thickens and is smooth.

Pour the sauce over the meat slices, sprinkle over the parsley and serve.

10 Servings

Beef and bean casserole

	Metric/UK	US
Dried black-eyed beans, soaked in cold water over night	450g/1lb	2⅔ cups
Cold water	1½l/2½ pints	6¼ cups
Salt and pepper		
Pork sausages	½kg/1lb	1lb
Cooking oil	1 Tbs	1 Tbs
Large onions, chopped	2	2
Garlic cloves, crushed	2	2
Stewing beef (beef chuck), cubed	1kg/2lb	2lb
Chopped fresh savory	1 tsp	1 tsp
Bay leaf	1	1
Chopped fresh marjoram	½ tsp	½ tsp
Large tomatoes, blanched, skinned and sliced	4	4
Beef stock or red wine	175ml/6floz	¾ cup

Drain the beans and transfer them to a large saucepan. Pour over the water and add salt and pepper to taste. Bring to the boil, reduce the heat to low and simmer for 1½ hours, or until the beans are cooked through and tender. Drain and reserve about 350ml/12floz (1½ cups) of the cooking liquid.

Preheat the oven to cool 150°C (Gas Mark 2, 300°F).

Slice the sausages into 2½cm/1in lengths. Heat the oil in a large frying-pan. Add the sausages and fry until they are evenly browned. Using a slotted spoon, transfer the sausages to drain on paper towels.

Pour off all but 3 tablespoons of the oil in the pan. Add the onions and garlic and fry until they are soft. Add the beef cubes and fry until they are evenly browned. Transfer the pan mixture to a large ovenproof casserole, and stir in the savory, bay leaf, marjoram, tomatoes and stock or wine. Season to taste, cover and put the casserole into the oven. Cook for 2 hours.

Remove the casserole from the oven and stir in the beans, sausage pieces

Beef and Bean Casserole is a hearty, filling dish, ideal for a family lunch on a cold winter's day.

and the reserved bean cooking liquid. Return to the oven and cook for a further 1 hour, stirring occasionally, or until the beef is cooked through and tender.

Remove from the oven and serve at once.

8 Servings

Marjoram beef ring

	Metric/UK	US
Minced (ground) beef	1kg/2lb	2lb
Fresh breadcrumbs	50g/2oz	1 cup
Salt and pepper		
Finely chopped fresh marjoram	2 Tbs	2 Tbs
Chopped fresh parsley	2 Tbs	2 Tbs
Small eggs, lightly beaten	2	2
Butter	25g/1oz	2 Tbs
Onion, finely chopped	1	1
SAUCE		
Vegetable oil	3 Tbs	3 Tbs
Small onion, finely chopped	1	1
Carrot, finely chopped	1	1
Small celery stalk, finely chopped	1	1
Flour	1 Tbs	1 Tbs
Beef stock	600ml/ 1 pint	2½ cups
Tomato purée (paste)	2 tsp	2 tsp
Bouquet garni	1	1
Madeira	75ml/3floz	⅜ cup

Preheat the oven to moderate 180°C (Gas Mark 4, 350°F). Lightly oil a large ring and set aside.

Put the beef, breadcrumbs, seasoning, herbs and eggs into a large bowl and beat until they are thoroughly mixed.

Melt the butter in a frying-pan. Add the onion and fry until it is soft, then stir into the beef mixture. Spoon the mixture into the prepared mould and put the mould into a deep roasting tin. Pour in enough hot water to come halfway up the sides of the mould. Place the tin in the oven and bake for 2 hours or until the beef mixture is lightly browned and comes away slightly from the side of the dish.

Meanwhile, to prepare the sauce, heat the oil in a small saucepan. Add the vegetables and fry until they are soft. Remove the pan from the heat and stir in the flour to form a smooth paste. Gradually add the stock, tomato purée (paste) and bouquet garni, return to the heat and bring to the boil, stirring constantly. Cook for 2 to 3 minutes, stirring constantly, or until the sauce thickens. Simmer for 20 minutes, stirring occasionally.

Strain the sauce into a bowl, pressing down on the vegetables with the back of a wooden spoon to extract all the liquid. Return the strained sauce to the saucepan, and bring to the boil. Stir in the Madeira, remove from the heat and keep warm.

When the meat loaf is cooked, remove from the oven and set aside in the mould for 5 minutes. Run a knife around the edge of the mould and turn the beef ring out on to a warmed serving dish. Serve at once, with the sauce.

6-8 Servings
NOTE: You can fill the centre of the ring with fresh minted peas, or sautéed mushrooms for a special effect.

Flank steak stew with herbs

	Metric/UK	US
Flank steak, cubed	1½kg/3lb	3lb
Seasoned flour (flour with salt and pepper to taste)	50g/2oz	½ cup
Butter	75g/3oz	6 Tbs
Vegetable oil	2 Tbs	2 Tbs
Medium onions, thinly sliced	3	3
Garlic cloves, crushed	3	3
Large green pepper, pith and seeds removed and chopped	1	1
Walnuts, finely chopped	50g/2oz	⅓ cup
Chopped fresh parsley	2 Tbs	2 Tbs
Chopped fresh oregano	1 tsp	1 tsp
Chopped fresh thyme	1 tsp	1 tsp
Bay leaves	2	2
Salt	1 tsp	1 tsp
Beef stock	450ml/ 15floz	2 cups
Tomato purée (paste)	2 Tbs	2 Tbs
Beurre manié (two parts flour and one part butter blended to a paste)	25g/1oz	2 Tbs

Coat the meat cubes in the seasoned flour, shaking off any excess.

Melt 50g/2oz (4 tablespoons) of the butter with the oil in a large saucepan. Add the meat cubes and fry until they are evenly browned. Using a slotted spoon, transfer the cubes to a plate. Add the remaining butter to the pan and add the onions, garlic and pepper. Fry until they are soft. Stir in the walnuts, herbs and salt and cook the mixture for 3 minutes, stirring occasionally. Add the stock and tomato purée (paste) and bring to the boil, stirring occasionally.

Return the meat cubes to the pan, reduce the heat to low and cover. Simmer for 2 hours, or until the meat is cooked through and tender. Add the beurre manié, a little at a time, and cook uncovered until the mixture

thickens and is smooth. Simmer for 5 minutes, stirring occasionally. Serve at once.

8 Servings

Beef with parsley dumplings

	Metric/UK	US
Stewing beef (beef chuck), cubed	1kg/2lb	2lb
Seasoned flour (flour with salt and pepper to taste)	40g/1½oz	⅓ cup
Butter	25g/1oz	2 Tbs
Cooking oil	1 Tbs	1 Tbs
Large onion, chopped	1	1
Bay leaf	1	1
Beef stock, hot	1¼l/2 pints	5 cups
Mushrooms, quartered	175g/6oz	1½ cups
Sour cream	150ml/5floz	⅔ cup
DUMPLINGS		
Fresh breadcrumbs	225g/8oz	4 cups
Water	50ml/2floz	¼ cup
Eggs, lightly beaten	3	3
Salt and pepper		
Chopped fresh parsley	1½ Tbs	1½ Tbs
Onion, finely chopped	1	1
Ground mace	½ tsp	½ tsp

Preheat the oven to warm 170°C (Gas Mark 3, 325°F).

Coat the beef cubes in the seasoned flour, shaking off any excess.

Melt the butter with the oil in a frying-pan. Add the onion and fry until it is soft. Add the beef cubes and fry until they are evenly browned. Using a slotted spoon, transfer the beef and onion to an ovenproof casserole. Add the bay leaf and hot stock, cover and put the casserole into the oven. Cook for 2 hours.

Meanwhile, to make the dumplings, put the breadcrumbs in a large bowl. Gradually stir in sufficient of the water so that the breadcrumbs are moist but not soggy. Gently beat in the remaining ingredients until the mixture is thoroughly blended. Using floured hands, shape the mixture into walnut-sized balls. Add the dumplings to the casserole, with the mushrooms, re-cover and cook for a further 30 minutes.

Remove from the oven and pour over the sour cream before serving.

6 Servings

Beef with Parsley Dumplings, mushrooms and sour cream is a substantial and satisfying main dish.

Lamb stew with dill

	Metric/UK	US
Butter	125g/4oz	8 Tbs
Lean lamb, cubed	1kg/2lb	2lb
Salt and pepper		
Garlic clove, crushed	1	1
Medium onion, finely chopped	1	1
Chopped fresh dill	3 Tbs	3 Tbs
Flour	50g/2oz	$\frac{1}{2}$ cup
Grated nutmeg	$\frac{1}{4}$ tsp	$\frac{1}{4}$ tsp
Chicken stock	600ml/1 pint	2$\frac{1}{2}$ cups
Large carrots, thinly sliced	2	2
Leeks, washed and thinly sliced	2	2
Double (heavy) cream	250ml/8floz	1 cup

Preheat the oven to moderate 180°C (Gas Mark 4, 350F).

Melt half the butter in a flameproof casserole. Add the meat and fry until the cubes are evenly browned. Stir in the seasoning, garlic, onion and dill. Cook until the onion is soft. Remove the casserole from the heat and stir in the flour to form a paste. Gradually stir in the nutmeg and stock. Return to the heat and bring to the boil, stirring constantly. Cover the casserole and put into the oven. Cook for 1 to 1$\frac{1}{4}$ hours, or until the meat is cooked through and tender.

Meanwhile, melt the remaining butter in a frying-pan. Add the vegetables and fry for 5 minutes, stirring occasionally. Remove from the heat. Remove the casserole from the oven and stir in the cream, then stir in about half the vegetable mixture. Transfer the stew to a warmed serving dish and garnish with the remaining vegetable mixture. Serve at once.

4-6 Servings

Lamb chops with thyme

	Metric/UK	US
Olive oil	50ml/2floz	$\frac{1}{4}$ cup
Lemon juice	2 Tbs	2 Tbs
Salt and pepper		
Chopped fresh thyme	1 Tbs	1 Tbs
Garlic clove, crushed	1	1
Thick lamb chops	4	4

Put the oil, lemon juice, seasoning, thyme and garlic into a shallow bowl and mix well. Add the lamb chops and baste well. Set aside in a cool place for 2 hours, basting frequently.

Preheat the grill (broiler) to high.

Arrange the chops on a rack in a lined grill (broiler) pan and cook for 2 minutes on each side. Reduce the heat to moderately low and cook the chops for a further 8 minutes on each side, basting them frequently with the marinade, or until they are cooked through and tender.

Transfer the chops to a warmed serving plate and spoon over the marinade. Serve at once.

4 Servings

Leg of lamb with rosemary

	Metric/UK	US
Leg of lamb	1x2kg/4lb	1x4lb
Garlic cloves, cut into 4 slices lengthways	2	2
Salt and pepper		
Dried rosemary	2 tsp	2 tsp
Butter	50g/2oz	4 Tbs
Beef stock	225ml/8floz	1 cup

Preheat the oven to fairly hot 200°C (Gas Mark 6, 400°F).

Lay the meat on a work surface and make eight deep incisions in it. Insert one garlic slice into each incision. Rub the meat all over with the salt, pepper and rosemary and set aside.

Melt the butter in a large roasting tin set over moderate heat. Add the meat and fry, turning frequently, for about 10 minutes or until it is lightly browned all over. Pour over the stock.

Transfer the roasting tin to the oven and roast the meat for 15 minutes. Reduce the heat to moderate 180°C (Gas Mark 4, 350°F) and roast the meat for a further 1$\frac{1}{2}$ hours or until the lamb is cooked through and tender. Transfer the meat to a warmed serving dish. Skim off any fat from the surface of the cooking juices, pour over the meat and serve immediately.

4 Servings

Saddle of lamb with rosemary

	Metric/UK	US
Saddle of lamb	1x2$\frac{3}{4}$kg/6lb	1x6lb
Salt and pepper		
Garlic cloves, cut into 8 slices	2	2
Rosemary sprigs	8	8
Flour, blended with 2 Tbs beef stock to a smooth paste	1 Tbs	1 Tbs
Beef stock	150ml/5floz	$\frac{2}{3}$ cup
MARINADE		
Red wine vinegar	50ml/2floz	$\frac{1}{4}$ cup
Olive oil	50ml/2floz	$\frac{1}{4}$ cup
Tomato purée (paste)	1 Tbs	1 Tbs
Fresh root ginger, peeled and finely grated	2$\frac{1}{2}$cm/1in piece	1in piece

Rub the meat all over with the salt and pepper. To make the marinade, put all the ingredients into a large, shallow dish and mix well. Add the meat to the marinade and set aside at room

The addition of rosemary and garlic to this dish gives Leg of Lamb with Rosemary a taste and aroma to tempt the most jaded palate. Serve with parsley potatoes and sauteed courgettes (zucchini) for a special family lunch or dinner party.

temperature for 3 hours, basting occasionally.

Preheat the oven to moderate 180°C (Gas Mark 4, 350°F).

Remove the lamb from the marinade and discard the marinade. Put the meat on a flat surface. Make eight deep incisions at intervals in the meat and insert one garlic slice and one rosemary sprig into each incision. Arrange the saddle on a rack in a deep roasting pan and put the pan into the oven. Roast for 1 hour. Reduce the oven temperature to cool 150°C (Gas Mark 2, 300°F) and roast for a further 1 to 1¼ hours, or until the lamb is cooked through and tender. Remove from the oven and transfer the lamb to a carving board. Carve into thick slices and transfer them to a warmed serving dish. Keep hot while you finish the sauce.

Remove the rack from the roasting pan and skim off any fat from the surface of the pan juices. Strain the juices into a small saucepan and stir in the flour mixture and stock. Set the pan over moderate heat and cook, stirring constantly, for 3 minutes, or until the sauce is smooth and has thickened. Pour into a warmed sauceboat and serve at once, with the meat.

8 Servings

Lamb and cashew nut curry

	Metric/UK	US
Fresh root ginger, peeled and chopped	4cm/1½in piece	1½in piece
Garlic cloves	3	3
Green chillis	2	2
Unsalted cashew nuts	50g/2oz	⅓ cup
Water	50-75ml/ 2-3floz	¼-⅓ cup
Cloves	4	4
Cardamom seeds	¼ tsp	¼ tsp
Coriander seeds	1 Tbs	1 Tbs
White poppy seeds	1 Tbs	1 Tbs
Butter	50g/2oz	4 Tbs
Onions, finely chopped	2	2
Lean lamb, cubed	1kg/2lb	2lb
Yogurt	300ml/10floz	1¼ cups
Saffron threads, soaked in 2 Tbs boiling water	¼ tsp	¼ tsp
Salt	1 tsp	1 tsp
Juice of ¼ lemon		
Chopped coriander leaves	1 Tbs	1 Tbs
Lemon, sliced	1	1

Put the ginger, garlic, chillis, nuts and half the water into a blender. Blend until it forms a purée. Add the cloves, cardamom, coriander and poppy seeds and blend with enough of the remaining water to make a smooth purée. Transfer the purée to a bowl.

Melt the butter in a large saucepan. Add the onions and fry until they are golden. Stir in the spice purée and reduce the heat to moderately low. Fry for 3 minutes, stirring frequently. Add the lamb cubes and fry until they are evenly browned.

Beat the yogurt, saffron and salt together, then pour the mixture into the saucepan. When the mixture begins to bubble, reduce the heat to low and simmer the curry for 1 hour, stirring occasionally.

Stir in the lemon juice and sprinkle over the coriander leaves. Cover the pan and cook for a further 20 minutes, or until the lamb is cooked through and tender.

Garnish with the lemon slices and serve at once.

4-6 Servings

Sage pork fillets

	Metric/UK	US
Pork fillet (tenderloin)	1kg/2lb	2lb
Salt and pepper		
Butter	50g/2oz	4 Tbs
Chopped fresh sage	2 Tbs	2 Tbs
Emmenthal (Swiss) cheese, cut into 12 slices	225g/8oz	8oz
French mustard	2 Tbs	2 Tbs
Single (light) cream	175ml/6floz	¾ cup

Rub the fillet all over with salt and pepper.

Melt the butter in a large saucepan. Add the fillet and sprinkle over the sage. Fry until the meat is deeply and evenly browned. Reduce the heat to low, cover the pan and simmer for 40 minutes, turning the meat occasionally. Remove from the heat. Using a slotted spoon, transfer the fillet to a chopping board. Make 12 deep incisions along the meat. Spread the cheese slices with three-quarters of the mustard and put one slice into each incision.

Carefully return the pork to the pan and set the pan over moderate heat. Cook for a further 5 to 10 minutes, or until the pork is cooked through and tender and the cheese has melted. Transfer the meat to a warmed serving dish. Carve into serving pieces and keep hot while you finish making the sauce.

Stir the remaining mustard into the pan juices. Pour in the cream and cook for a further 1 minute, stirring constantly, until the sauce is hot but not boiling. Pour the sauce into a warmed sauceboat and serve at once, with the meat.

6 Servings

French pork pie

	Metric/UK	US
Puff pastry, chilled	350g/12oz	3 cups
Egg yolk, lightly beaten	1	1
FILLING		
Lean pork, minced (ground)	1kg/2lb	2lb
Brandy	50ml/2floz	¼ cup
Butter	1 Tbs	1 Tbs
Vegetable oil	2 Tbs	2 Tbs
Shallots, finely chopped	2	2
Garlic clove, crushed	1	1
Finely chopped fresh sage	1 Tbs	1 Tbs
Finely chopped fresh parsley	1 Tbs	1 Tbs
Finely chopped fresh chervil	1 Tbs	1 Tbs
Salt and pepper		
Cornflour (cornstarch) mixed to a paste with 1 Tbs water	1 Tbs	1 Tbs

First prepare the filling. Place the pork in a large shallow dish. Pour over the brandy and set aside to marinate for at least 1 hour.

Meanwhile, melt the butter with the oil in a large frying-pan. Add the shallots and garlic until the shallots are soft. Add the pork and brandy to the pan and fry, stirring frequently, until the pork is lightly browned. Add the herbs and salt and pepper to taste. Cook, stirring occasionally, for a further 15 minutes.

Remove the pan from the heat and stir in the cornflour (cornstarch) mixture. Set aside.

Preheat the oven to hot 220°C (Gas Mark 7, 425°F).

Divide the dough in half. Roll out one half into a circle large enough to line a greased 23cm/9in pie plate. Lift the dough on to one plate and press gently into position. Trim off any excess dough and add the filling, doming it up in the centre. Moisten the edges of the dough with a little water.

Roll out the remaining dough in the

Lamb and Cashew Nut Curry is a delicately flavoured dish which may be served with rice and chappatis for an authentic Indian meal.

Marinated with garlic and thyme, Pork with Peaches has a sweet and scrumptious flavour.

same way and lift it on to the filling. Trim the edges and crimp them together. Cut a fairly large cross in the middle of the dough. Roll out the trimmings and make decorative shapes. Press the shapes on to the dough and brush with the beaten egg yolk.

Place the plate in the oven and bake for 5 minutes. Reduce the heat to moderate 180°C (Gas Mark 4, 350°F) and continue baking for a further 30 minutes or until the pastry is a deep golden brown.

Remove the plate from the oven and serve either hot or cold.

6 Servings

Pork with peaches

	Metric/UK	US
Leg of pork	1x2¾kg/6lb	1x6lb
Salt		
White wine vinegar	225ml/8floz	1 cup
White wine	225ml/8floz	1 cup
Ground allspice	1 tsp	1 tsp
Ground cinnamon	½ tsp	½ tsp
Canned peach halves, drained	12	12
Cornflour (cornstarch) mixed to a paste with		
1 Tbs peach can juice	1 Tbs	1 Tbs
MARINADE		
Olive oil	125ml/4floz	½ cup
Garlic cloves, crushed	2	2
Salt and pepper		
Prepared French mustard	1 tsp	1 tsp
Finely chopped fresh thyme	1 tsp	1 tsp

First make the marinade. Combine all the ingredients in a large shallow dish. Add the pork and leave to marinate for 2 hours, basting occasionally.

Preheat the oven to fairly hot 190°C (Gas Mark 5, 375°F).

Remove the pork from the marinade and place it on a working surface. Discard the marinade. Make small incisions in the thickest part of the flesh, then rub salt in the skin.

Put the pork on a rack in a roasting tin and roast for 2½ to 3 hours or until the meat is cooked through and tender. Test by inserting the sharp point of a knife into the thickest part of the flesh. If the juices run clear then the meat is cooked.

Meanwhile, pour the vinegar and white wine into a small saucepan and place over low heat. Stir in the allspice and cinnamon. Simmer for 30 minutes, then remove the pan from the heat.

Place the peach halves in a large shallow dish and pour the vinegar and wine mixture over them. Set aside.

When the pork is cooked, transfer

it to a large warmed serving dish. Remove the peach halves from the vinegar and wine mixture and arrange them around the pork. Reserve the vinegar and wine mixture. Keep the pork hot while you make the sauce.

Skim the excess fat from the top of the cooking juices in the roasting tin, then pour the juices into a saucepan and place over moderate heat. Add the reserved vinegar and wine mixture and bring to the boil. Reduce the heat to low, add the cornflour (cornstarch) mixture and cook, stirring constantly, for 2 to 3 minutes or until the sauce has thickened. Pour the sauce into warmed sauceboat.

Serve the pork immediately with the sauce.

6-8 Servings

Juniper pork chops

	Metric/UK	US
Large pork chops	4	4
Garlic cloves, halved	2	2
Salt and pepper		
Juniper berries, crushed	20	20
Olive oil	4 Tbs	4 Tbs

Preheat the grill (broiler) to high.

Rub each chop all over with half a garlic clove, then with salt and pepper to taste. Gently press the juniper berries into both sides of the meat.

Arrange the chops on a rack in a lined grill (broiler) pan and brush with oil. Reduce the heat to moderate and grill (broil) the chops for about 10 minutes on each side, or until the meat is cooked through and tender.

Transfer the chops to a warmed serving dish and serve at once.

4 Servings

Stuffed loin of pork

	Metric/UK	US
Loin of pork, boned	1x2kg/4lb	1x4lb
Liver pâté	175g/6oz	6oz
Chopped fresh sage	2 tsp	2 tsp
Garlic cloves, crushed	2	2
Salt and pepper		
Fresh white breadcrumbs	50g/2oz	1 cup
Egg, lightly beaten	1	1
Mushrooms, thinly sliced	125g/4oz	4oz
Vegetable oil	1 Tbs	1 Tbs

Preheat the oven to fairly hot 190°C (Gas Mark 5, 375°F).

Place the pork, skin side up, on a working surface and score the skin into thin parallel slices ½cm/¼-inch apart. Turn the pork over.

In a bowl, mix together the pâté, sage, garlic, salt and pepper to taste, breadcrumbs and egg. Spread the mixture over the meat to within 3cm/1in of the edges. Top with the sliced mushrooms, roll up Swiss (jelly) roll style and tie with string.

Rub more salt into the scored skin and brush with the vegetable oil. Put the meat on a rack in a roasting tin and roast for 2½ hours, or until the meat is cooked through and tender. To test, insert the sharp point of a knife into the flesh. If the juices run clear then the meat is cooked.

Increase the heat to hot, 220°C (Gas Mark 7, 425°F), and roast for a further 20 minutes or until the skin is crisp. Remove and discard the string, transfer to a warmed serving dish and serve immediately.

8 Servings

Loin of veal with herb stuffing

	Metric/UK	US
Boned loin of veal, trimmed of excess fat	1x2¾kg/6lb	1x6lb
Salt	2 tsp	2 tsp
Black pepper	1 tsp	1 tsp
Egg yolks	2	2
Double (heavy) cream	3 Tbs	3 Tbs
Fresh white breadcrumbs	75g/3oz	1½ cups
Onion, grated	1	1
Finely chopped fresh chives	1 Tbs	1 Tbs
Finely chopped fresh parsley	1 Tbs	1 Tbs
Finely chopped fresh sage	1 Tbs	1 Tbs
Finely chopped fresh marjoram	½ Tbs	½ Tbs
Finely grated rind and juice of 2 oranges		
Butter	50g/2oz	4 Tbs
Streaky (fatty) bacon	8 slices	8 slices
Beurre manié (two parts flour to one part butter, blended to a paste)	1 Tbs	1 Tbs
Orange, thinly sliced	1	1
Watercress sprigs to garnish		

Preheat the oven to fairly hot 190°C (Gas Mark 5, 375°F).

Rub the veal all over with half the salt and the pepper. Place it, fat side down, on a flat surface.

Beat the egg yolks, cream, breadcrumbs and remaining salt and pepper together until the mixture forms a smooth paste. Stir in the onion, herbs and orange rind. Spoon the mixture on to the veal and spread to within about 2½cm/1in of the edges of the meat. Roll the meat up and tie securely with string at 2½cm/1in intervals. Set aside.

Melt the butter in a large flameproof casserole. Add the veal roll and fry until it is evenly browned. Lay the bacon slices over the top of the roll, cover the casserole and put into the centre of the oven. Braise for 2½ to 3 hours, or until the veal is cooked through and tender. Remove from the oven and, using two large forks, transfer the meat to a carving board. Remove the string and bacon and carve the meat into thick slices. Arrange on a warmed serving dish and keep the meat hot while you make the sauce.

Skim off any fat from the surface of the casserole juices. Set the casserole over moderate heat and stir in the orange juice. Add the beurre manié, a little at a time, and cook until the sauce has thickened. Strain the sauce into a sauceboat and serve at once. Garnish the meat with the orange slices and watercress sprigs and serve at once, with the sauce.

10-12 Servings

Veal escalopes with tarragon sauce

	Metric/UK	US
Veal escalopes, pounded thin	4	4
Seasoned flour (flour with salt and pepper to taste)	40g/1½oz	⅓ cup
Butter	75g/3oz	6 Tbs
Tomatoes, blanched, skinned and sliced	2	2
Button mushrooms, sliced	125g/4oz	1 cup
Chopped fresh tarragon	1 Tbs	1 Tbs
Salt and pepper		

Coat the escalopes in the seasoned flour, shaking off any excess.

Melt two-thirds of the butter in a large frying-pan. Add the escalopes and fry for 4 to 6 minutes on each side, or until they are cooked through and tender. Transfer them to a plate and keep the chops warm while you cook the vegetables.

Melt the remaining butter in the pan. Add the tomatoes and mushrooms, and fry until they are soft. Stir in the tarragon and seasoning and simmer for 3 minutes.

Return the escalopes to the pan and baste with the vegetable mixture. Simmer for 5 minutes.

Serve at once.

4 Servings

A superb dish of veal stuffed with herbs and orange rind and then braised slowly in the oven, Loin of Veal with Herb Stuffing makes a stunning dinner party dish.

Sweetbreads with cheese

	Metric/UK	US
Sweetbreads, soaked in cold water for 3 hours, drained, skinned and trimmed	½kg/1lb	1lb
Onion, sliced	1	1
Chopped fresh tarragon	2 tsp	2 tsp
Chopped fresh chervil	2 tsp	2 tsp
Chopped fresh parsley	1 Tbs	1 Tbs
Bay leaf	1	1
Salt and pepper		
Dry white wine	300ml/10floz	1¼ cups
Butter	50g/2oz	4 Tbs
Flour	25g/1oz	¼ cup
Cheddar cheese, grated	175g/6oz	1½ cups

Place the sweetbreads in a large saucepan and cover with water. Bring the water to the boil, remove the pan from the heat and set aside for 10 minutes.

Remove the sweetbreads and drain on paper towels. Discard the water. Cut the sweetbreads into 1cm/½in slices.

Place the sweetbreads, onion, herbs, salt and pepper in a bowl. Pour over the wine and leave to marinate for 30 minutes.

Using a slotted spoon, remove the sweetbreads from the marinade and drain on paper towels. Strain the marinade into a bowl and discard the contents of the strainer.

Melt half the butter in a frying-pan. Add the sweetbreads and fry, turning occasionally, for 10 to 15 minutes or until they are lightly browned.

Transfer the sweetbreads to a shallow flame-proof dish and keep them hot while you make the sauce.

Preheat the grill (broiler) to high.

Melt the remaining butter in a small saucepan. Remove the pan from the heat and stir in the flour to make a smooth paste. Gradually stir in the marinade. Return the pan to the heat and bring the sauce to the boil, stirring constantly. Cook the sauce for 2 to 3 minutes or until the sauce is thick and smooth.

Add half of the cheese and stir constantly until it has melted. Pour the sauce over the sweetbreads and sprinkle over the remaining cheese.

Place the dish under the grill (broiler) for 5 minutes or until the cheese has melted and is golden brown. Serve at once.

3 Servings

An exceptionally tasty dish, Liver and Sausage Kebabs consists of bite-sized pieces of liver, chipolata sausages, mushrooms, tomatoes and bay leaves threaded on skewers and quickly grilled (broiled). Serve the kebabs on a bed of rice and accompany with a mixed green salad.

Liver and sausage kebabs

	Metric/UK	US
Calf's liver	½kg/1lb	1lb
Small chipolata (skinless) sausages	½kg/1lb	1lb
Butter, melted	175g/6oz	12 Tbs
Black pepper		
Button mushrooms	225g/8oz	2 cups
Bay leaves	24	24
Large tomatoes, quartered, or 24 tiny (cherry) tomatoes	6	6

Preheat the grill (broiler) to moderate.

Cut the liver into 2½cm/1in cubes. Leave the sausages whole if they are very small, otherwise halve them.

Pour half the melted butter into a shallow bowl and roll the liver cubes in it, then season with pepper to taste.

Thread the liver, sausages, mushrooms, bay leaves and tomatoes or tomato quarters on to skewers, in alternating order. Brush with half the remaining melted butter.

Arrange the skewers on a rack in a lined grill (broiler) pan and cook for 6 to 8 minutes on each side, or until the meat is cooked through and tender, brushing occasionally with the remaining melted butter.

Transfer the skewers to a warmed serving dish and serve at once.

4 Servings

Kidneys, Dijon-style

	Metric/UK	US
Butter	15g/½oz	1 Tbs
Vegetable oil	1 Tbs	1 Tbs
Lambs' kidneys, skinned, cored and cut into large pieces	675g/1½lb	1½lb
Flour	2 Tbs	2 Tbs
Milk	300ml/10floz	1¼ cups
French mustard	2-3 Tbs	2-3 Tbs
Salt and pepper		
Chopped fresh parsley	4 Tbs	4 Tbs

Melt the butter with the oil in a large deep frying-pan. Add the kidney pieces and fry until they are deeply and evenly browned. Using a slotted spoon, transfer them to a plate.

Stir the flour into the liquid in the pan to form a smooth paste. Gradually add the milk and bring to the boil, stirring constantly. Stir in the mustard, seasoning and all but 1 tablespoon of the parsley and simmer gently for 5 minutes.

Return the kidney pieces to the pan and baste well with the sauce. Simmer for 2 to 3 minutes, or until they are cooked through and tender. Sprinkle over the remaining parsley and serve at once.

4 Servings

Tomato tripe casserole

	Metric/UK	US
Tripe, blanched	1kg/2lb	2lb
Large onions, quartered	2	2
Carrots, thickly sliced	2	2
Bouquet garni	1	1
Salt and pepper		
Chicken stock	900ml/1½ pints	3¾ cups
Vegetable oil	2 Tbs	2 Tbs
Canned peeled tomatoes	700g/1½lb	1½lb
Tomato purée (paste)	2 Tbs	2 Tbs
Sugar	2 tsp	2 tsp
Garlic cloves, crushed	2	2
Chopped fresh basil	1 Tbs	1 Tbs
Chopped fresh parsley	3 Tbs	3 Tbs
Squeeze of lemon juice		
Grated cheese	3 Tbs	3 Tbs
Dry white breadcrumbs	2 Tbs	2 Tbs
Butter	15g/½oz	1 Tbs

Preheat the oven to warm 170°C (Gas Mark 3, 325°F).

Cut the tripe into 5cm/2in squares and lay them in a flameproof casserole. Add the onions, carrots and bouquet garni, and sprinkle over salt and pepper to taste. Pour over the stock, cover and bake in the over for 1 hour.

Meanwhile, heat the oil in a saucepan and add the tomatoes and can juice. Stir in the tomato purée (paste),

sugar, garlic and herbs. Cook over moderate heat for about 10 minutes, stirring occasionally, or until the liquid has thickened. Taste and flavour with lemon juice and adjust the seasoning. Set aside.

Strain the tripe, discard the carrots and bouquet garni and reserve the cooking liquid. Chop the onions and add them to the tomato sauce with the tripe.

Return the tripe and tomato mixture to the casserole and bring to the boil. Cover, return to the oven and bake for a further 1 hour, or until the tripe is tender.

Increase the heat to 190°C (Gas Mark 5, 375°F). Uncover the casserole and sprinkle with the cheese and breadcrumbs and dot with the butter, cut into small dice. Return to the oven and bake until the cheese is golden and bubbling. Serve immediately.

4 Servings

Tripe, much praised by Samuel Pepys and the people of Caen, is one of the cheapest foods you can buy and can be mouth-wateringly delicious. Tomato Tripe Casserole is a particularly good dish which consists of a combination of cheese, tomatoes, herbs and tripe.

VEGETABLES & SALADS

Broad beans with savory

	Metric/UK	US
Vegetable oil	2 Tbs	2 Tbs
Onion, finely chopped	1	1
Garlic clove, crushed	1	1
Chopped fresh parsley	1 Tbs	1 Tbs
Chopped fresh savory	1 tsp	1 tsp
Chopped fresh lovage	½ tsp	½ tsp
Broad (lima or fava) beans, soaked overnight in cold water and drained	1kg/2lb	5 cups
Chicken stock	600ml/1 pint	2½ cups
Salt and pepper		
Grated nutmeg	½ tsp	½ tsp
Sour cream	250ml/8floz	1 cup

Heat the oil in a large saucepan. Add the onion and garlic and fry until they are soft. Add the herbs and beans and cook for 2 minutes. Add the stock, seasoning to taste and nutmeg and bring to the boil. Reduce the heat to low, cover the pan and simmer for 1 to 1½ hours, or until the beans are tender.

Drain off any excess liquid and stir in the sour cream. Serve at once.

6-8 Servings

Baked potatoes with sour cream and chives

	Metric/UK	US
Large potatoes, scrubbed	4	4
Salt and pepper		
Butter	50g/2oz	4 Tbs
Sour cream	250ml/8floz	1 cup
Chopped fresh chives	2-3 Tbs	2-3 Tbs

Preheat the oven to fairly hot 200°C (Gas Mark 6, 400°F).

Prick the potatoes with a fork and then arrange them on a baking sheet, or wrap them in aluminium foil. Put them into the oven and bake for 1 to 1¼ hours, depending on the size of the potatoes (the tops should be soft to the touch when the potatoes are cooked.)

Remove the potatoes from the heat and arrange them in a serving dish. Make a deep incision across the tops of the potatoes and scoop out a little of the potato flesh from each one. Transfer the flesh to a bowl. Season the potatoes, salt and pepper to taste and add a dollop of butter. Set aside.

Beat the sour cream and chives into the bowl with the potato flesh until they are well blended. Spoon the sour cream mixture back into the baked potatoes and serve at once.

4 Servings

Potato salad

	Metric/UK	US
Potatoes, cooked and sliced	½kg/1lb	1lb
Mayonnaise	125ml/4floz	½ cup
Lemon juice	1 Tbs	1 Tbs
Olive oil	1 Tbs	1 Tbs
Salt and pepper		
Chopped fresh chives	2 Tbs	2 Tbs
Chopped leeks	4 Tbs	4 Tbs

Put three-quarters of the potatoes into a bowl. Add the mayonnaise, lemon juice, oil, seasoning and half the chives. Using two large spoons, carefully toss until the potatoes are thoroughly coated.

Spoon the mixture into a serving bowl. Arrange the remaining potato slices over the top of the salad and sprinkle with the remaining chives. Scatter the leeks around the edge of the bowl.

Cover the bowl and put into the refrigerator to chill for 30 minutes before serving.

4 Servings

Artichoke hearts with herbs

	Metric/UK	US
Water	900ml/1½pts	3¾ cups
Lemon juice	2 Tbs	2 Tbs
Salt	1 tsp	1 tsp
Fresh artichoke hearts	12	12
Butter	40g/1½oz	3 Tbs
Chopped fresh chervil	1 tsp	1 tsp
Chopped fresh parsley	½ tsp	½ tsp

Bring the water to the boil in a saucepan. Add the lemon juice and salt and reduce the heat to moderately low. Carefully arrange the artichoke hearts in the water and simmer for 10 minutes. Remove from the heat, transfer the hearts to a plate and leave until they are cool enough to handle. Cut them into thin slices.

Melt the butter in a frying-pan. Add the artichoke hearts and fry gently for

This simple Potato Salad with mayonnaise dressing may be served with cold meats or as one of a selection of salads. Use the green part of the leeks for this recipe and save the white parts for future use.

130

Quick and easy to prepare, Aniseed Carrots is an unusual and delicately flavoured vegetable dish.

about 1 minute, turning them at least once. Transfer the slices and any remaining butter to a warmed serving dish and sprinkle over the chervil and parsley.

Serve at once.

4 Servings

Salsify sautéed with butter and herbs

	Metric/UK	US
Butter	25g/1oz	2 Tbs
Garlic clove, crushed	1	1
Salsify, trimmed, boiled, drained and peeled	½kg/1lb	1lb
Chopped fresh chervil	1 tsp	1 tsp
Finely chopped fresh parsley	2 Tbs	2 Tbs
Salt and pepper		
Lemon juice	1 tsp	1 tsp

Melt the butter in a frying-pan. Add the garlic and fry for 1 minute, stirring constantly. Add the chervil, parsley, salt and pepper and cook, stirring constantly, for 6 to 8 minutes, or until the salsify is lightly browned. Pour over the lemon juice. Transfer the salsify to a warmed serving dish and serve immediately.

4 Servings

Aniseed carrots

	Metric/UK	US
Soft brown sugar	1 Tbs	1 Tbs
Butter	50g/2oz	4 Tbs
Aniseed	1½ tsp	1½ tsp
Salt and pepper		
Carrots, quartered if large, whole if small	700g/1½lb	1½/lb

Put the sugar, butter, aniseed and seasoning into a large saucepan. When the butter and sugar have melted, add the carrots. Stir well, reduce the heat to low and cover the pan. Simmer for 15 minutes, or until the carrots are tender.

Transfer the mixture to a warmed serving dish and serve at once.

4 Servings

Chervil and avocado salad

	Metric/UK	US
Ripe avocados, peeled and stoned (pitted)	4	4
Lemon juice	125ml/4floz	½ cup
Salt and pepper		
Chopped fresh chervil	1 Tbs	1 Tbs

Cut the avocados, lengthways, into long, thin slices and arrange them in a shallow glass dish. Pour over the lemon juice and season to taste. Cover and marinade the avocado in the

refrigerator for 1 hour.

Remove from the refrigerator and, using a slotted spoon, transfer the avocado slices to a chilled serving dish. Discard the lemon juice. Sprinkle over the chervil.

Serve at once.

4 Servings

Salsify with tarragon sauce

	Metric/UK	US
Salsify, cleaned	½kg/1lb	1lb
Toasted breadcrumbs	1 Tbs	1 Tbs
SAUCE		
Butter	25g/1oz	2 Tbs
Flour	2 Tbs	2 Tbs
Milk	125ml/4floz	½ cup
Chicken stock	125ml/4floz	½ cup
Single (light) cream	125ml/4floz	½ cup
Salt and pepper		
Grated nutmeg	½ tsp	½ tsp
Finely chopped fresh tarragon	2 tsp	2 tsp

Cut the salsify into 8cm/3in lengths and put them into a bowl of cold water with a little vinegar added (they will turn brown otherwise). Half-fill a large saucepan with water and bring to the boil. Add the salsify and cook over moderate heat for 20 minutes, or until it is tender. Drain and keep hot while you make the sauce.

Melt the butter in a saucepan.

Remove from the heat and stir in the flour to form a smooth paste. Gradually add the milk, stock and cream and return the pan to the heat. Cook, stirring constantly, for 2 to 3 minutes, or until the sauce is smooth and has thickened and is hot but not boiling. Stir in the seasoning, nutmeg and tarragon and simmer for a further 3 minutes.

Arrange the salsify in a warmed, deep serving dish. Pour over the sauce and sprinkle over the breadcrumbs. Serve at once.

4 Servings

Baked tomatoes with basil

	Metric/UK	US
Butter	75g/3oz	6 Tbs
Large onions, thinly sliced into rings	2	2
Large tomatoes, blanched, skinned and thinly sliced	10	10
Chopped fresh basil	2 Tbs	2 Tbs
Salt and pepper		
Sugar	1 tsp	1 tsp
Fresh breadcrumbs	75g/3oz	1½ cups

Preheat the oven to fairly hot 200°C (Gas Mark 6, 400°F).

Melt a third of the butter in a frying-pan. Add the onion rings and fry until they are soft. Remove the pan from the heat.

Arrange a layer of onion rings over the bottom of a well-greased medium baking dish. Cover with a layer of tomato slices, generously sprinkled with basil, seasoning and sugar. Cut about 1 tablespoon of the remaining butter into dice and scatter over. Repeat the layers until all the ingredients are used up.

Top with the breadcrumbs. Cut the remaining butter into dice and scatter over the breadcrumbs.

Put the dish into the oven and bake for 30 minutes, or until the top is browned and bubbling slightly. Serve at once.

4-6 Servings

Pizza Margherita

(Pizza with Basil, Tomatoes and Cheese)
This pizza is positively patriotic—the three main colours of the filling (green, red and white), are intended to represent the colours of the Italian flag.

	Metric/UK	US
Fresh yeast	15g/½oz	½oz
Sugar	¼ tsp	¼ tsp
Lukewarm water	125ml/4floz plus 3 tsp	½ cup plus 3 tsp
Flour	225g/8oz	2 cups
Salt	1 tsp	1 tsp
FILLING		
Tomatoes, thinly sliced	6	6
Mozzarella cheese, sliced	175g/6oz	6oz
Chopped fresh basil	2 Tbs	2 Tbs
Salt and pepper		
Olive oil	2 tsp	2 tsp

Crumble the yeast into a small bowl and mash in the sugar. Add the 3 teaspoons of water and cream the mixture. Set aside in a warm, draught-free place for 15 to 20 minutes, or until the mixture is puffed up and frothy.

Sift the flour and salt into a large, warmed bowl. Make a well in the centre and pour in the yeast mixture and the remaining lukewarm water. Using a spatula, gradually draw the flour into the liquid until it is all incorporated and the dough comes away from the sides of the bowl.

Turn the dough out on to a floured surface and knead for about 10 minutes. The dough should be elastic and smooth.

Rinse, dry and lightly grease the bowl. Shape the dough into a ball and return it to the bowl. Cover and set aside in a warm, draught-free place for 45 minutes to 1 hour, or until the dough has risen and almost doubled in bulk.

Preheat the oven to very hot 230°C (Gas Mark 8, 450°F).

Turn the dough out on to the floured surface and knead for 3 minutes. Cut the dough in half and roll out each piece into a circle, about ½cm/¼in thick. Arrange the circles, well spaced apart, on a well-greased baking sheet. Arrange the tomato slices in decorative lines over each circle, and separate them with overlapping Mozzarella slices. Sprinkle the basil generously over the top and season to taste. Dribble over the oil.

Put the sheet into the oven and bake for 15 to 20 minutes, or until the dough is cooked through and the cheese has melted. Serve at once.

2 Servings

Ratatouille

(Mixed Vegetable Casserole)

	Metric/UK	US
Butter	25g/1oz	2 Tbs
Olive oil	50ml/2floz	¼ cup
Large onions, thinly sliced	2	2
Garlic cloves, crushed	2	2
Medium aubergines (eggplants), thinly sliced and dégorged	3	3
Large green pepper, pith and seeds removed and chopped	1	1
Large red pepper, pith and seeds removed and chopped	1	1
Medium courgettes (zucchini), sliced	5	5
Canned peeled tomatoes	425g/14oz	14oz
Chopped fresh basil	2 tsp	2 tsp
Chopped fresh rosemary	2 tsp	2 tsp
Salt and pepper		
Chopped fresh parsley	2 Tbs	2 Tbs

Melt the butter with the oil in a large saucepan. Add the onions and garlic and fry until they are soft. Add the aubergine (eggplant) slices, peppers and courgette (zucchini) slices, and fry for 5 minutes, shaking the pan frequently. Add the tomatoes and can juice, herbs, salt and pepper and sprinkle over the parsley. Bring to the boil. Reduce the heat to low, cover the pan and simmer for 40 to 45 minutes, or until the vegetables are tender but still firm.

Serve hot or cold.

6 Servings

Vegetable rissoles

	Metric/UK	US
Red lentils, soaked in cold water overnight, cooked and drained	125g/4oz	½ cup
Large onion, finely chopped	1	1
Celery stalk, finely chopped	1	1
Small carrots, grated	2	2
Green beans, cooked and finely chopped	50g/2oz	⅓ cup
Fresh white breadcrumbs	50g/2oz	1 cup
Eggs	3	3
Salt and pepper		
Chopped fresh mixed herbs	1 Tbs	1 TPs
Vegetable oil	50ml/2floz	¼ cup

Put the lentils, vegetables, fresh breadcrumbs, 2 of the eggs, the seasoning and mixed herbs into a bowl and beat until thoroughly blended. Set aside at room temperature for 30 minutes.

Using your hands, shape the mixture into eight equal-sized balls, then flatten to make small cakes. Set aside.

Beat the remaining egg in a shallow dish, and put the dry breadcrumbs on a plate. Dip each rissole first in the eggs, then the breadcrumbs, coating them completely and shaking off any excess.

Heat the vegetable oil in a large frying-pan. Add the rissoles and fry for 10 minutes on each side, or until they

Pizza Margherita is extremely patriotic as the colours of the filling ingredients, basil, tomatoes and Mozzarella cheese, echo those of the Italian flag: green, red and white.

135

are golden brown. Remove from the pan and drain on paper towels. Serve at once.

4 Servings

Tomato salad with chives and basil

	Metric/UK	US
Firm tomatoes, thinly sliced	$\frac{1}{2}$kg/1lb	1lb
Finely chopped fresh chives	1 Tbs	1 Tbs
Finely chopped fresh basil	2 tsp	2 tsp
DRESSING		
Olive oil	3 Tbs	3 Tbs
White wine vinegar	1 Tbs	1 Tbs
Lemon juice	$\frac{1}{2}$ tsp	$\frac{1}{2}$ tsp
French mustard	$\frac{1}{4}$ tsp	$\frac{1}{4}$ tsp
Salt and pepper		
Chopped fresh basil	$\frac{1}{2}$ tsp	$\frac{1}{2}$ tsp

Arrange the tomato slices decoratively on a salad plate and sprinkle over the chives. Set aside.

To make the dressing, put all the ingredients into a screw-top jar, cover and shake well. Dribble the dressing over the tomato slices.

Sprinkle over the basil and serve at once.

4 Servings

Coleslaw with caraway

	Metric/UK	US
Large white cabbage, cored and shredded	1	1
Medium onion, finely chopped	1	1
Green pepper, pith and seeds removed and Finely chopped	2	2
Lemon juice	$\frac{1}{2}$ tsp	$\frac{1}{2}$ tsp
Caraway seeds	1 Tbs	1 Tbs
DRESSING		
Double (heavy) cream	175ml/6floz	$\frac{3}{4}$ cup
Sour cream	75ml/3floz	$\frac{1}{3}$ cup
French mustard	1 Tbs	1 Tbs
Lemon juice	3 Tbs	3 Tbs
Sugar	1 Tbs	1 Tbs
Salt and pepper		

Arrange the cabbage in a large serving dish and sprinkle with the onion, pepper and lemon juice. Set aside.

To make the dressing, beat all the ingredients together until they are thoroughly mixed. Pour the dressing over the cabbage mixture and add the caraway seeds. Using two large spoons, gently toss the mixture until the cabbage is thoroughly coated. Put the bowl into the refrigerator to chill for at least 1 hour before serving.

8 Servings

Walnut and rice salad

	Metric/UK	US
Large firm tomatoes	6	6
Walnuts, halved	175g/6oz	$1\frac{1}{3}$ cups
Cooked long-grain rice	215g/7$\frac{1}{2}$oz	3 cups
Cooked ham, diced	350g/12oz	12oz
Green beans, cooked and drained	225g/8oz	$1\frac{1}{3}$ cups
Sultanas or seedless raisins	125g/4oz	$\frac{2}{3}$ cup
Canned sweetcorn, drained	425g/14oz	14oz
Chopped fresh basil	2 tsp	2 tsp
Chopped fresh sage	1 tsp	1 tsp
French dressing	50ml/2floz	$\frac{1}{4}$ cup
GARNISH		
Walnut halves	12	12
Chopped fresh parsley	1 Tbs	1 Tbs

Put the tomatoes on a board and cut off the tops. Discard the tops, then scoop out and discard the seeds, taking care not to pierce the skins. Set the tomato shells aside.

Put all the remaining ingredients, except the garnish, into a bowl and mix together until they are thoroughly combined. Using two large spoons, toss the salad until all the ingredients are well coated.

Fill the tomatoes with the rice mixture and arrange them around the edge of a serving dish. Spoon the remaining rice mixture into the centre. Garnish with the walnut halves and parsley and serve at once.

6 Servings

Herb and spinach flan

	Metric/UK	US
Shortcrust pastry	175g/6oz	$1\frac{1}{2}$ cups
FILLING		
Butter	50g/2oz	4 Tbs
Small onion, thinly sliced into rings	1	1
Lean bacon slices, chopped	3	3
Spinach, trimmed and cooked	$\frac{1}{2}$kg/1lb	1lb
Eggs, lightly beaten	2	2
Double (heavy) cream	150ml/5floz	$\frac{2}{3}$ cup
Salt and pepper		
Chopped fresh thyme	2 tsp	2 tsp
Chopped fresh basil	1 tsp	1 tsp
Chopped fresh parsley	1 Tbs	1 Tbs
Cheddar cheese, grated	50g/2oz	$\frac{1}{2}$ cup

Preheat the oven to fairly hot 200°C (Gas Mark 6, 400°F).

Roll out the pastry dough on a flat surface to about $\frac{1}{2}$cm/$\frac{1}{4}$in thick, then use to line a 23cm/9in flan ring. Put the flan ring on to a baking sheet and set aside.

To make the filling, melt the butter in a large frying-pan. Add the onion and fry until it is soft. Add the bacon and fry for 5 minutes, or until it is crisp. Stir in the spinach and cook until the spinach is heated through. Remove the pan from the heat and spoon the mixture into the prepared pastry shell.

Beat the eggs, cream, seasoning and herbs together until they are thoroughly blended. Stir in the cheese and mix well. Pour the mixture over the spinach and put the baking sheet into the oven. Bake for 30 minutes, or until the filling is set and the top has browned.

Serve hot or cold.

4-6 Servings

Garlic potatoes

The number of garlic cloves given below is NOT a mistake—nor will you be fearsome to be near for hours after eating this delicious dish! Once the cloves have been boiled they lose their strength, but retain a pleasant taste.

	Metric/UK	US
Potatoes, quartered	1½kg/3lb	3lb
Salt	1½ tsp	1½ tsp
Garlic cloves, peeled	25	25
Butter	25g/1oz	2 Tbs
Flour	1 Tbs	1 Tbs
Double (heavy) cream	250ml/8floz	1 cup
Black pepper		
Finely chopped fresh chives	1 Tbs	1 Tbs

Put the potatoes into a large saucepan and sprinkle with 1 teaspoon of salt. Cover with water and set the pan over moderate heat. Bring to the boil and cook for 20 minutes, or until the potatoes are tender.

Meanwhile, put the garlic cloves in a saucepan and cover with water. Bring to the boil and boil briskly for 3 minutes. Remove from the heat and drain the garlic. Grind the cloves or blend them to a smooth purée.

Melt the butter in a saucepan. Add the garlic and cook for 5 minutes, stirring frequently. Remove from the heat and stir in the flour to form a smooth paste. Gradually add the cream and return the pan to the heat. Cook for 2 minutes, stirring constantly, or until the sauce is thick and smooth and hot but not boiling. Stir in the remaining salt, pepper to taste and the chives. Set aside.

Drain the potatoes, then mash them well. Rub them through a strainer and return the puréed potatoes to the saucepan. Gradually beat in the garlic and cream sauce. Set the pan over moderate heat and cook, stirring constantly, for 2 to 3 minutes, or until the mixture is reheated.

Serve at once.

10 Servings

Coleslaw with Caraway is a crunchy combination of shredded cabbage, onion and green pepper topped with a sour cream, mustard, lemon juice and caraway seed dressing.

SAUCES, STUFFINGS & STOCKS

Below

1 *For Béarnaise Sauce, strain the simmered vinegar mixture into a small bowl, cream the butter until it is soft and beat the egg yolks in a third ovenproof bowl.*

2 *Place the bowl of egg yolks over a pan filled with warm water, or use a double boiler, and add the butter mixture in small pieces, stirring constantly.*

3 *Having stirred in the vinegar, remove the bowl from the pan and add the pepper, tarragon and chervil.*

Opposite page The use of home-made Beef Stock (see page 143) will add a touch of distinction to soups and casseroles.

Béarnaise sauce

	Metric/UK	US
Wine vinegar	5 Tbs	5 Tbs
Shallot or small onion, quartered	1	1
Bay leaf	1	1
Tarragon sprig	1	1
Chervil sprig	1	1
Peppercorns	4	4
Butter	125g/4oz	8 Tbs
Large egg yolks	2	2
Salt and pepper		
Chopped fresh mixed tarragon and chervil	1 tsp	1 tsp

Put the vinegar, shallot or onion, herbs and peppercorns into a small saucepan. Simmer until the vinegar is reduced to about 1 tablespoon. Strain and set aside. Discard the contents of the strainer.

Beat the butter until it is soft. Beat the egg yolks in a second, oven-proof bowl until they are thoroughly blended. Add a heaped teaspoon of the butter and salt to the egg yolks and cream thoroughly. Stir in the vinegar.

Put the bowl in a saucepan containing warm water and set the pan over low heat. (The water should heat gradually but should not be allowed to boil.) Add the remaining butter in small pieces, stirring constantly. When all the butter has been added and the sauce is the consistency of whipped cream, add the pepper, chopped tarragon and chervil. Taste and adjust seasoning if necessary.

About 150ml/5floz ($\frac{5}{8}$ cup)

Béchamel sauce

	Metric/UK	US
Milk	450ml/ 15floz	2 cups
Bay leaf	1	1
Peppercorns	6	6
Pinch of grated nutmeg		
Butter	2 Tbs	2 Tbs
Flour	25g/1oz	$\frac{1}{4}$ cup
Salt and white pepper		

Put the milk, bay leaf, peppercorns and nutmeg into a saucepan. Simmer for 10 minutes, taking care not to let the milk come to the boil. Strain the milk into a bowl and set aside.

Melt the butter in a saucepan.

Remove the pan from the heat and stir in the flour to form a smooth paste. Gradually add the infused milk. Return the pan to the heat and season to taste. Bring to the boil, then cook for 2 to 3 minutes, stirring constantly, or until the sauce thickens and is smooth.

About 450ml/15floz (2 cups)

Bergamot sauce

	Metric/UK	US
Butter	25g/1oz	2 Tbs
Shallots, finely chopped	2	2
Flour	1 Tbs	1 Tbs
Dry white wine	125ml/4floz	$\frac{1}{2}$ cup
Juice of $\frac{1}{2}$ lemon		
Chopped fresh bergamot	1 Tbs	1 Tbs
Salt and white pepper		

Melt the butter in a small saucepan. Add the shallots and fry until they are soft. Stir in the flour to form a smooth paste. Gradually add the wine and lemon juice, stirring constantly, and cook for 2 to 3 minutes, or until the sauce thickens and is smooth. Stir in the bergamot and seasoning and simmer for a further 2 minutes, stirring constantly.

Pour into a warmed sauceboat and serve hot.

About 125ml/4floz ($\frac{1}{2}$ cup)

Mint sauce

This is the classic British accompaniment to roast leg of lamb.

	Metric/UK	US
Finely chopped fresh mint	12 Tbs	12 Tbs
Sugar	1$\frac{1}{2}$ Tbs	1$\frac{1}{2}$ Tbs
Malt or distilled white vinegar	75ml/3floz	6 Tbs
Hot water	1 Tbs	1 Tbs

Pound the mint and sugar together in a mortar with a pestle, or mix them in a bowl with a wooden spoon. Add the vinegar and hot water and stir until the sugar has dissolved.

Set aside for 1 hour before serving.

About 175ml/6floz ($\frac{3}{4}$ cup)

Tomato sauce with herbs

	Metric/UK	US
Tomatoes, blanched, skinned, seeded and chopped	½kg/1lb	1lb
Olive oil	1 Tbs	1 Tbs
Onion, finely chopped	1	1
Garlic clove, crushed	1	1
Bouquet garni	1	1
Chopped fresh marjoram	2 tsp	2 tsp
Sugar	1 tsp	1 tsp
Salt and pepper		

Put all the ingredients into a saucepan and bring to the boil. Reduce the heat to low and simmer for 25 to 30 minutes, or until the liquid has reduced a little and the sauce thickened.

Remove from the heat and remove and discard the bouquet garni. Strain the sauce into a warmed sauceboat or jug and adjust the seasoning if necessary. Serve at once.

About 150ml/5floz (¾ cup)

Pesto sauce

This classic sauce is made from fresh sweet basil and pine nuts and is usually served over spaghetti. Noodles, however, could be substituted if you prefer them.

	Metric/UK	US
Garlic cloves, crushed	2	2
Finely chopped fresh basil	50g/2oz	½ cup
Finely chopped pine nuts	3 Tbs	3 Tbs
Salt	½ tsp	½ tsp
Pepper to taste		
Olive oil	250ml/8floz	1 cup
Grated Parmesan cheese	50g/2oz	½ cup

Crush the garlic, basil, pine nuts and seasoning in a mortar until the mixture forms a smooth paste. Gradually pound in the oil, then the cheese, until the sauce is thick and smooth.

Pour the sauce over spaghetti or noodles and toss until the pasta is thoroughly coated. Serve at once.

4-6 Servings

Tarragon butter

	Metric/UK	US
Butter	125g/4oz	8 Tbs
Lemon juice	1 Tbs	1 Tbs
Chopped fresh tarragon	2-3 Tbs	2-3 Tbs
Salt and white pepper		

Beat the butter with a wooden spoon until it is soft and creamy. Drop by drop, beat the lemon juice into the butter, then beat in tarragon and salt

Below Pesto is a classic Genoese sauce which is marvellous with all pasta dishes and as a flavouring for soups. Bottom left To make Tarragon Butter, having creamed the butter first, gradually add the lemon juice, seasoning and tarragon. Beat until there are no droplets of lemon juice visible on the surface. Bottom right Fines Herbes Vinaigrette is a piquant salad dressing flavoured with fresh herbs and mustard. Stir well to emulsify.

and pepper to taste.
Chill until firm.

Fines herbes vinaigrette
(Herb Salad Dressing)

	Metric/UK	US
Finely chopped fresh chervil	½ tsp	½ tsp
Finely chopped fresh chives	1 tsp	1 tsp
Finely chopped fresh parsley	1 Tbs	1 Tbs
French mustard	1 tsp	1 tsp
Salt and pepper		
Garlic clove, crushed	1	1
Olive oil	175ml/6floz	¾ cup
Tarragon vinegar	50ml/2floz	¼ cup
Lemon juice	2 tsp	2 tsp

Put the herbs, mustard, seasoning and garlic into a small bowl and beat well. Gradually stir in the oil. Pour the mixture into a screw-top jar and add the remaining ingredients. Cover and shake well. The vinaigrette is now ready to be used.

About 250ml/8floz (1 cup)

French dressing

The ingredients for French dressing and the proportion of vinegar to oil are very largely a matter of personal taste, but this is a good basic recipe which will give enough dressing to toss a salad for four people. Try using a herb-flavoured oil or vinegar (see page 36) for a variation in flavour, or add a clove of crushed garlic. French dressing can be stored for a month in a cool place and it is a good idea to make up a large quantity so that you always have some on hand.

	Metric/UK	US
Mustard, dry	¼ tsp	¼ tsp
Salt and black pepper		
Sugar	¼ tsp	¼ tsp
Wine vinegar	1 Tbs	1 Tbs
Olive oil	2 Tbs	2 Tbs

Put the mustard, seasoning to taste, sugar and vinegar into a bowl and

beat well. Stir in the oil. Alternatively, put all the ingredients into a screw-top jar and shake well. The dressing is now ready to be used.

50ml/2floz (¼ cup)

Ravigote butter

This classic butter is traditionally used to garnish steaks, or any other grilled (broiled) meats, but it also makes a flavouring for sauces and casseroles.

	Metric/UK	US
Butter	50g/2oz	4 Tbs
Finely chopped fresh chives	1 Tbs	1 Tbs
Finely chopped fresh parsley	1 Tbs	1 Tbs
Finely chopped fresh chervil	1 Tbs	1 Tbs
Finely chopped fresh tarragon	1 Tbs	1 Tbs
Garlic clove, crushed	1	1

Beat the butter with a wooden spoon until it is soft and creamy. Beat in the herbs and garlic until the mixture is well blended.

Cover and chill in the refrigerator for 1 hour, or until firm.

Herb and orange stuffing

This stuffing can be used to stuff lamb duck or goose, but it is especially good with chicken. The quantity given below is enough to fill a 2½kg/5lb chicken.

	Metric/UK	US
Butter	25g/1oz	2 Tbs
Large onion, very finely chopped	1	1
Lean veal, minced (ground)	½kg/1lb	1lb
Fresh white breadcrumbs	175g/6oz	3 cups
Salt and pepper		
Finely grated rind of 1 orange		
Chopped fresh marjoram	2 tsp	2 tsp
Chopped fresh thyme	1 tsp	1 tsp
Finely chopped fresh chives	1 Tbs	1 Tbs
Double (heavy) cream	2 Tbs	2 Tbs
Orange juice	50ml/2floz	¼ cup

Melt the butter in a saucepan. Add the onion and fry until it is soft. Add the veal and fry until it loses its pinkness. Stir in the breadcrumbs, seasoning, orange rind and herbs and cook the mixture for 5 minutes, stirring constantly.

Stir in the cream and orange juice until the mixture is thoroughly combined. The stuffing is now ready.

About 575g/1¼lb

Sage and onion stuffing

This traditional stuffing is excellent with poultry, or even pork. The quantity given below is enough to fill a 1½kg/3lb chicken.

	Metric/UK	US
Large onions, finely chopped	2	2
Chopped fresh sage leaves	12	12
Fresh white breadcrumbs	125g/4oz	2 cups
Salt and pepper		
Melted butter	1 Tbs	1 Tbs
Egg yolk	1	1

Half-fill a saucepan with water and set over high heat. When the water boils, add the onions. Reduce the heat to low, cover the pan and simmer for 10 minutes, or until the onions are tender. Remove from the heat and strain the mixture. Discard the water.

Put the onions into a small bowl. Stir in the sage, breadcrumbs and seasoning, and mix well. Stir in the melted butter and egg yolk until the stuffing is thoroughly combined. The stuffing is now ready to be used.

About 225g/8oz

Note: If you do not wish to use the stuffing immediately, cover and store in the refrigerator and do not add the butter and egg yolk until just before the stuffing is required.

Thyme stuffing

This stuffing is excellent with poultry, veal or even fish. The quantity given below is enough to fill a 1½kg/3lb chicken, or fish.

	Metric/UK	US
Fresh white breadcrumbs	125g/4oz	2 cups
Eating apples, peeled, cored and finely chopped	2	2
Medium onion, finely chopped	1	1
Sultanas or seedless raisins	75g/3oz	½ cup
Finely chopped fresh thyme	2 tsp	2 tsp
Finely chopped fresh lemon thyme	2 tsp	2 tsp
Salt and pepper		
Egg, lightly beaten	1	1

Put all the ingredients into a bowl and stir until the stuffing is thoroughly combined. If the mixture is still slightly crumbly, add a little water or lemon juice. The stuffing is now ready to be used.

About 225g/8oz

Rosemary Jelly is an apple and vinegar based condiment flavoured with sprigs of fresh rosemary. It is the ideal accompaniment to roast meats, especially lamb and veal.

Rosemary jelly

This savoury jelly is usually served with meat, particularly lamb and veal dishes. You will need about 450g/1lb (2 cups) of granulated sugar per 600ml/1 pint (2½ cups) of strained apple juice.

	Metric/UK	US
Cooking apples, sliced	2½kg/5lb	5lb
Water	600ml/	
	1 pint	2½ cups
Fresh rosemary leaves	4 Tbs	4 Tbs
Malt vinegar	250ml/8floz	1 cup
Granulated or preserving sugar		
Green food colouring	6 drops	6 drops

Scald a jelly bag or cheesecloth by pouring boiling water through it into a large bowl. Hang the bag or cheesecloth on a frame or tie the ends to the legs of an upturned chair or stool and place a large bowl underneath.

Put the apples and water in a large saucepan and stir in half of the rosemary. Bring to the boil, reduce the heat to low and simmer the fruit for 40 to 50 minutes, or until it is soft and pulpy. Add the vinegar and boil for 5 minutes.

Pour the mixture into the bag or cloth and leave to drain through for at least 12 hours. Do not squeeze the bag to hurry the process as this will make the jelly cloudy. When the juice has completely drained through, discard the pulp remaining in the bag or cheesecloth.

Measure the juice before returning it to the rinsed-out pan. Add 450g/1lb (2 cups) of sugar to each 600ml/1 pint (2½ cups) of liquid. Set the pan over low heat and stir until the sugar has dissolved. Increase the heat to high and bring to the boil. Boil briskly, without stirring, for about 10 minutes, or until the jelly has reached setting point. (To test, remove the pan from the heat and spoon a little jelly on to a cold saucer. Cool quickly. If the surface is set and wrinkles when pushed with your finger, it is set; if setting point has not been reached return to the heat and continue boiling, testing frequently.)

Skim the foam from the surface of the jelly with a metal spoon. Sprinkle the remaining rosemary and food colouring over the jelly and stir well.

Ladle the jelly into hot, clean, dry jam jars, leaving 1cm/½in space at the top. Wipe with a damp cloth, cover and secure the covers with rubber bands. Label the jars and store in a cool, dry place until ready to use.

About 2kg/4lb

Beef stock

	Metric/UK	US
Beef shin bone, cut into pieces	1kg/2lb	2lb
Marrow bone	1	1
Water	3½l/6 pints	7 pints
Large onion, halved	1	1
Carrots, chopped	2	2
Large leek, washed thoroughly and halved	1	1
Celery stalk, halved	1	1
Peppercorns	8	8
Cloves	4	4
Bouquet garni	1	1
Salt	1 Tbs	1 Tbs

Put the bones into a large saucepan. Add the water and bring slowly to the boil, skimming any scum from the surface. Continue to remove the scum until it stops rising.

When the scum stops rising, add the remaining ingredients and cover the pan. Simmer gently for 4 hours, or until the liquid has reduced by about half.

Strain the stock through a strainer lined with two layers of cheesecloth. If you are going to use the stock immediately, cool it and remove the fat. If you are storing it, leave the fat intact.

About 1¾l/3 pints (7½ cups)

Chicken stock

	Metric/UK	US
Carcass, bones and giblets (excluding the liver) of a cooked or raw chicken		
Carrot, sliced	1	1
Celery stalks, sliced	4	4
Onion, stuck with 2 cloves	1	1
Bouquet garni	1	
Grated rind of ½ lemon		
Salt	1 tsp	1 tsp
Peppercorns	10	10
Water	1¾l/3pints	7½ cups

Put the carcass, bones and giblets (if available) into a large saucepan. Add the vegetables, bouquet garni, lemon rind, salt, peppercorns and water and bring to the boil, skimming any scum from the surface as it rises. Half-cover the pan, reduce the heat to low and simmer for 2 hours.

Remove the pan from the heat and strain the stock into a bowl. If you are going to use the stock immediately, cool it and remove the fat. If you are storing it, leave the fat intact.

About 1½l/2½ pints (6¼ cups)

The use of home-made stocks in soups and casseroles can make an enormous difference to their flavour. Simple and cheap to make, they will keep for several days in a refrigerator and months in a freezer.
1 Put the chicken carcass, giblets and vegetables into a large saucepan.
2 Add water, lemon rind and seasoning, and, to give it a special flavour, a bouquet garni. Tying the bouquet garni to the handle will facilitate its easy removal.
3 After the stock has cooked, strain into a bowl and discard the contents of the strainer. If you are going to use the stock immediately, cool it and remove the fat.

PUDDINGS & DESSERTS

Pineapple upside down cake

	Metric/UK	US
Butter	150g/5oz	10 Tbs
Soft brown sugar	2 Tbs	2 Tbs
Medium fresh pineapple, peeled, cored and cut into 9 rings, or 425g/14oz canned pineapple rings, drained	1	1
Glace (candied) cherries	9	9
Sugar	125g/4oz	½ cup
Eggs	2	2
Self-raising flour, sifted	175g/6oz	1½ cups
Milk	3 Tbs	3 Tbs
Angelica, cut into 18 leaves	5cm/2in piece	2in piece

Preheat the oven to moderate 180°C (Gas Mark 4, 350°F). Lightly grease a 20cm/8in square cake tin. Cut 25g/1oz (2 tablespoons) of the butter into small pieces and dot them over the base of the tin. Sprinkle the brown sugar over the top. Arrange the pineapple slices decoratively on top of the sugar and put a cherry in the centre of each ring. Set aside.

Beat the remaining butter with a wooden spoon until it is soft and creamy. Add the sugar and beat until the mixture is light and fluffy. Add the eggs, one at a time, beating well until they are thoroughly blended. Fold in the flour. Stir in enough of the milk to give the batter a dropping consistency.

Spoon the batter into the baking tin, being careful not to dislodge the cherries. Put the tin into the oven and bake for 50 minutes to 1 hour, or until a skewer inserted into the centre of the cake comes out clean. Remove the tin from the oven and set aside to cool for 5 minutes. Run a knife around the sides of the cake and invert on to a serving dish. Decorate each cherry with two angelica leaves.

Serve the cake warm, or set aside to cool completely before serving.

9 Servings

Crystallized angelica

Crystallized angelica is expensive to buy because the process of crystallizing is time consuming. If you do the crystallizing yourself you can afford to use angelica more liberally. It is difficult to estimate the quantity that this recipe will make as the amount will vary according to the thickness of the stalks used. As well as adding crystallized angelica to cakes, it is an attractive way of adding flavour and colour to home-made candies and hot milk.

	Metric/UK	US
Angelica, stalks and leaves removed, cut into 15cm/6in lengths	225g/8oz	8oz
Sugar	450g/1lb	2 cups
Water	600ml/1pint	2½ cups
Icing (confectioners') sugar		

Cook the stalks in boiling water until they give slightly when pressed with the fingers.

Plunge the stalks in icy water to refresh and, as soon as they are cold, drain and thinly peel away any stringy fibres.

Stir the sugar into the water over low heat until dissolved. Bring to the boil. Lay the angelica stalks in a shallow heatproof dish and pour over the boiling sugar syrup. Cover and leave to soak for 24 hours.

Drain the syrup off the angelica and reheat to 110°C (225°F), then pour it over the angelica again. Cover and set aside for a further 24 hours. Repeat this process for two further consecutive days.

On the fourth day, heat the syrup to 120°C (245°F) and add the angelica. Bring to the boil three or four times. This is to stop the syrup bubbling over and to allow the angelica to absorb it. Set aside until cool. Lift the pieces of angelica out of the syrup onto a wire rack and set aside until the surface is dry.

Preheat the oven to very cool 110°C (Gas Mark 1, 275°F).

Roll the dry pieces of angelica in icing (confectioners') sugar. Place on a baking sheet and put in the oven until dried through. (The amount of time this takes varies according to the thickness of the angelica stalks.) The surface should not be sticky to the touch when the angelica is thoroughly dried.

Wrap in greaseproof or waxed paper and store in bottles in a cool dark place until needed.

Opposite page *Pineapple Upside-down cake is a popular American cake which makes a splendid and filling dessert. The fruit and the angelica, which gives the cake colour as well as taste, are arranged in the bottom of the cake tin and the batter poured over the top. When the cake is baked, it is turned out, upside-down, to display the fruit. Below The addition of Crystallized Angelica to desserts and cakes adds both to their appearance and taste. As it is expensive to buy we have included this recipe so that you can make it yourself from the angelica plants in your own garden to ensure a constant and cheap supply throughout the year.*

Suédoise
(Fruit Jelly [Gelatine] Mould)

	Metric/UK	US
Large eating apple, peeled, cored and thinly sliced	1	1
Lemon juice, blended with 2 Tbs water	2 tsp	2 tsp
Maraschino cherries	6	6
Blanched almonds	6	6
Angelica leaves	12	12
Fresh apricots, halved, stoned (pitted) and poached	½kg/1lb	1lb
Fresh plums, halved, stoned (pitted) and poached	½kg/1lb	1lb
JELLY (GELATIN)		
Boiling water	900ml/ 1½ pints	3¾ cups
Sugar	225g/8oz	1 cup
Gelatine, dissolved in 4 Tbs boiling water	25g/1oz	1oz
Orange-flavoured liqueur	125ml/4floz	½ cup

First make the jelly (gelatin). Pour the water into a large bowl. Add the sugar and stir until it has dissolved. Stir in the gelatine mixture and liqueur. Set aside to cool. Chill the mixture in the refrigerator until the jelly (gelatin) is on the point of setting.

Meanwhile, combine the apple slices and lemon juice mixture and set aside.

Rinse a straight-sided 1½l/2½ pint (1½ quart) mould with water. Pour enough of the jelly (gelatin) mixture into the mould to make a ½cm/¼in layer on the bottom. Arrange the cherries, almonds and angelica leaves decoratively over it, remembering that the pattern will be the other way up when the dish is served. Spoon a little jelly (gelatin) over the pattern and place the mould in the refrigerator for 15 minutes, or until it has set. Remove from the refrigerator.

Arrange half the apricots over the jelly (gelatin) and spoon enough jelly (gelatin) to cover them completely. Chill the mould in the refrigerator for a further 30 minutes, or until it is set. Continue making layers in this way, using up the remaining apricots, the plums and apple slices, until all the ingredients are used up. Chill in the refrigerator for a final 2 hours, or until the mould has completely set.

Remove from the refrigerator and quickly dip the bottom into hot water. Place a chilled serving dish over the mould and invert the two, giving a sharp shake. The jelly (gelatin) should slide out easily.

4-6 Servings

A pretty French dessert, Suédoise is made with alternating layers of fresh fruit, nuts and angelica set in liqueur-flavoured jelly (gelatin). Serve with whipped cream.

Coriander fruit crumble

	Metric/UK	US
Cooking apples, peeled, cored and thinly sliced	700g/1½lb	1½lb
Blackberries	225g/8oz	8oz
Brown sugar	2 Tbs	2 Tbs
Ground cinnamon	1 tsp	1 tsp
TOPPING		
Flour	175g/6oz	1½ cups
Sugar	175g/6oz	¾ cup
Butter	175g/6oz	¾ cup
Ground coriander	2 tsp	2 tsp

Preheat the oven to moderate 180°C (Gas Mark 4, 350°F).

Put the apples and blackberries into a medium baking dish and sprinkle over the sugar and cinnamon.

To make the topping, put the flour and sugar into a bowl. Add the butter, cut into small dice, and rub the butter into the flour until the mixture resembles breadcrumbs. Mix in the coriander.

Sprinkle the topping mixture over the fruit, to cover it completely. Put the dish into the oven and bake for 45 minutes. Serve at once.

6 Servings

Verbena and apricot sherbet

	Metric/UK	US
Apricots, halved and stoned (pitted)	700g/1½lb	1½lb
Dried or fresh verbena leaves	8	8
Water	450ml/15floz	2 cups
Sugar	225g/8oz	1 cup
Gelatine, dissolved in 2 Tbs boiling water	15g/½oz	½oz
Double (heavy) cream	125ml/4floz	½ cup
Egg whites, stiffly beaten	2	2

Set the thermostat of the refrigerator to its coldest setting.

Put the apricots, verbena leaves water and sugar into a saucepan. Cover and bring to the boil. Reduce the heat to low and simmer the mixture until the apricots are tender and soft. Remove from the heat and set aside to cool.

Using a slotted spoon, transfer the apricots to a blender and blend until they form a smooth purée. Transfer the purée to a bowl. Add the apricot syrup and gelatine to the bowl and,

The inclusion of ground coriander in the crunchy topping of Coriander Fruit Crumble gives this dessert an attractive aroma and flavour.

A traditional British dessert, Tansy Apples is quick to make and delightful to eat — especially when served with sugar and cream.

using a wire whisk or rotary beater, whisk the mixture for 2 to 3 minutes, or until it is well blended. Cover and put into the refrigerator to chill for 1 hour.

When the mixture is cold, spoon it into a cold freezing tray and put it into the frozen food storage compartment of the refrigerator for 1 hour.

Meanwhile, beat the cream until it is thick but not stiff. Fold in the egg whites.

Remove the tray from the refrigerator and scrape the sherbet into a large bowl. Fold in the cream and egg white mixture. Beat the sherbet until it is smooth, then spoon back into the tray. Return the tray to the freezing compartment and freeze for 6 hours, or until the sherbet is firm to the touch.

Remove from the freezing compart-ment. Dip a serving spoon into hot water, then spoon the sherbet into individual glasses. Serve at once.

6 Servings

Gooseberry cream with elderflowers

	Metric/UK	US
Gooseberries, trimmed	½kg/1lb	1lb
Dried elderflowers	1 Tbs	1 Tbs
Water	300ml/	
	10floz	1¼ cups
Dry white wine	125ml/4floz	½ cup
Grated rind of 1 lemon		
Sugar	125g/4oz	½ cup
Eggs, separated	3	3

Put the gooseberries, elderflowers, water, wine and lemon rind into a saucepan and bring to the boil. Reduce

Tansy apples

	Metric/UK	US
Butter	25g/1oz	2 Tbs
Eating apples, peeled, cored and sliced	2	2
Eggs, lightly beaten	2	2
Double (heavy) cream	150ml/5floz	$\frac{2}{3}$ cup
Chopped fresh tansy	2 tsp	2 tsp
Grated lemon rind	$\frac{1}{2}$ tsp	$\frac{1}{2}$ tsp
Grated nutmeg	$\frac{1}{4}$ tsp	$\frac{1}{4}$ tsp
Fresh white breadcrumbs	2 Tbs	2 Tbs

The addition of elderflowers to this dessert, with their pleasant, sweet and distinctive flavour, makes Gooseberry Cream with Elderflowers a delicious end to any meal.

the heat to low and simmer, stirring occasionally, for 20 minutes, or until the gooseberries are soft. Remove the pan from the heat. Rub the mixture through a strainer into a bowl, discarding any pulp in the strainer. Rinse and dry the saucepan.

Return the purée to the saucepan and add the sugar. Set the pan over low heat and stir the mixture until the sugar has dissolved. Remove from the heat. Beat the egg yolks into the mixture, then set aside to cool to lukewarm.

Beat the egg whites until they form stiff peaks. Fold the egg whites into the mixture, then transfer it to a large bowl or individual serving glasses. Set aside in a cool place for 1 hour, or until the cream has set. Serve at once.

4 Servings

Melt the butter in a large frying-pan. Add the apple slices and fry, turning and stirring occasionally, until they are tender.

Meanwhile, beat the eggs, cream, tansy, lemon rind, nutmeg and breadcrumbs until they are well mixed.

Preheat the grill (broiler) to high.

Pour the egg mixture into the frying-pan, reduce the heat to low and cook the mixture for 10 minutes, or until it is almost firm to the touch. Do not stir. Remove from the heat and put under the grill (broiler) for 3 minutes or until the mixture is golden brown. Remove from the heat.

Cut into wedges and serve at once.

4-6 Servings

149

BREADS & CAKES

Rosemary bread

	Metric/UK	US
Fresh yeast	15g/½oz	½oz
Sugar	½ tsp	½ tsp
Lukewarm water	300ml/10floz	1¼ cups
Flour	350g/12oz	3 cups
Salt	1 tsp	1 tsp
Wholemeal (wholewheat) flour	125g/4oz	1 cup
Finely chopped fresh rosemary	3 Tbs	3 Tbs
Dried rosemary	1 tsp	1 tsp

Crumble the yeast into a small bowl and mash in the sugar. Add a tablespoon of the water and cream to the mixture. Set aside in a warm, draught-free place for 15 to 20 minutes, or until the mixture is puffed up and frothy.

Sift the flour and salt into a large warmed bowl. Stir in the wholemeal (wholewheat) flour and the fresh rosemary. Make a well in the centre and pour in the yeast mixture and remaining water. Using a spatula, gradually draw the flours into the liquid until they are all incorporated and the dough comes away from the sides of the bowl.

Turn the dough out on to a floured surface and knead it for about 5 minutes. The dough should be elastic and smooth.

Rinse, dry and lightly grease the bowl. Shape the dough into a ball and return it to the bowl. Cover and set aside in a warm, draught-free place for 1 to 1½ hours, or until the dough has risen and almost doubled in bulk.

Turn the dough out on to the floured surface and knead for about 3 minutes. Shape into a loaf and arrange in a well-greased ½kg/1lb loaf

An unusual accompaniment to cheese or soup, Rosemary Bread is particularly good served warm from the oven and spread with butter.

tin. Return to the warm, draught-free place for 30 to 45 minutes, or until the dough has risen to the top of the tin.

Preheat the oven to very hot 240°C (Gas Mark 9, 475°F).

Sprinkle the top of the bread with the dried rosemary and put the tin into the oven. Bake for 15 minutes. Reduce the oven temperature to fairly hot 190°C (Gas Mark 5, 375°F) and bake for a further 25 minutes, or until the bread is baked. (If the bread sounds hollow when you rap the undersides, then it is cooked; if not, return to an oven preheated to warm 170°C (Gas Mark 3, 325°F) and bake for a further 10 minutes.)

Cool the loaf before serving.

½kg/1lb Loaf

Aniseed and sesame biscuits (cookies)

	Metric/UK	US
Vegetable oil	350ml/ 12floz	1½ cups
Thinly pared rind of ½ lemon		
Aniseed	1 Tbs	1 Tbs
Sesame seeds	1 Tbs	1 Tbs
Dry white wine	125ml/4floz	½ cup
Fnely grated lemon rind	2 tsp	2 tsp
Finely grated orange rind	2 tsp	2 tsp
Sugar	125g/4oz	½ cup
Flour	575g/1¼lb	5 cups
Ground cinnamon	1 tsp	1 tsp
Ground cloves	1 tsp	1 tsp
Ground ginger	1 tsp	1 tsp
Blanched slivered almonds	25g/1oz	2 Tbs

Heat the oil in a saucepan. When it is hot, add the pared lemon rind, aniseed and sesame seeds and remove the pan from the heat. Set aside to cool. Remove and discard the lemon rind. Pour the oil mixture into a bowl and add the wine, lemon and orange rind and sugar, stirring until the sugar has dissolved.

Sift the flour and spices into a bowl. Gradually add the flour mixture to the oil, beating constantly until all the flour has been added and a stiff dough formed. Using your hands, lightly knead the dough until it is smooth. Form into a ball, wrap in greaseproof or waxed paper and set aside at room temperature for 30 minutes.

Preheat the oven to fairly hot 200°C (Gas Mark 6, 400°F). Line two large baking sheets with non-stick silicone paper and set aside.

Remove the paper from the dough and divide it into 24 equal pieces. Roll each piece into a small ball using the palms of your hands, then flatten them into flat, round biscuits (cookies), about 1cm/½in thick. Arrange the biscuits (cookies) on the baking sheets and press a few slivered almonds into each one.

Put the sheets into the oven and bake for 15 to 20 minutes, or until the biscuits (cookies) are firm to the touch and golden around the edges. Transfer the biscuits (cookies) to a wire rack to cool. Cool completely before serving.

24 biscuits (cookies)

Aniseed and Sesame Biscuits have a delightful flavour and will keep for up to two weeks if stored in an airtight tin.

151

INDEX

Picture Credits
A-Z Botanical Collection 72(tr); D. Arminson 76(r); Barnaby's Picture Library 93(b); Walter Bauer 57; Carlo Bevilacque 77; Steve Bicknell 4, 19(b), 21(I & br), 27, 34, 36, 42; Bodleian Library 10, 14(b); Brian Lake Books 51(t); Camera Press 43, 47, 135; Colonial Williamsburg 44; A. Cooke 63(b); R. J. Corbin 25(c), 35(t), 69(r), 86(r); J. Cowley 86(c); C. Dawkins 52(t); Delu PAF/International 105; Anthony Denney 23, 55(br), 140(tl); J. Downard 63(c); Alan Duns 25(b), 107, 108, 110, 120, 128, 140(br), 142, 150; Mary Evans 7(b), 9(tr & I); Derek Fell 74(tr); V. Finnis 19(t), 45, 46(t), 49(t), 63(t); Brian Furner 64(t); P. Genereux 29; Melvin Grey 129, 140(bl); Graeme Harris 24, 28; P. Hunt 89(c); A. J. Huxley 66; G. Hyde 13(b), 51(b), 55(bl), 60; Jacana 74(tl); L. Johns 54; Paul Kemp 103, 109, 113(b), 149; Don Last 117; David Lewin 143; Chris Lewis 40; Maison de Marie Claire/Godeaut 17; Mansell Collection 8, 12, 25(tr), 26, 52(b), 53; J. Markham 14(t), 15, 72(tl); Bill McLaughlin 2/3, 38; David Meldrum 119, 137, 138; Keith Morris Title verso; H. Morrison 84(t); Key Nilson 131; M. Nimmo 69(bl); S. J. Orme 69(tl); Pharmaceutical Society of Great Britain 96(r); Roger Phillips 37, 64(b), 99, 100/1, 104, 113(t), 114, 126, 132, 133, 139, 144, 145, 147, 148/9; Iain Reid 125, 146; Royal Horticultural Society 55(t), 56, 58, 61 62, 65, 67, 68, 70, 71, 73, 75, 78(r), 79, 80(t), 82, 83, 85, 87, 88, 90, 92, 94; Red Saunders 123; Scala 11; Harry Smith Horticultural Photographic Agency 21(tr), 22, 69(r), 76(I), 80(b), 84(b), 89(I); Snark 7(t); Tourist Photo Library 78(I); M. Warren 93(t); Michael Wickham 46(l & b); C. Williams 35(b); D. Woodland 59; George Wright 106;